Shelter & Shade
Creating a healthy and profitable environment for your livestock with trees

Shelter & Shade
Creating a healthy and profitable environment for your livestock with trees

by
John and Bunny Mortimer

with a foreword and North American notes
by Allan Nation

A division of Mississippi Valley Publishing, Corp.
Jackson, Mississippi

This 1996 edition is excerpted with special arrangement from **Trees for the New Zealand Countryside, A Planter's Guide** by John and Bunny Mortimer originally published in New Zealand by Taitua Books in 1984.

Illustrations by Ines Stäger and Jane Mortimer
Cover Design by Heritage Graphics, Jackson, MS

Library of Congress Cataloging-in-Publication Data

Mortimer, John, 1924-
[Trees for the New Zealand Countryside. Selections.] Shelter & Shade: Creating a healthy and profitable environment for your livestock with trees / by John and Bunny Mortimer ; with a foreword and North American Notes by Allan Nation.
p. cm.
"Excerpted with special arrangement from Trees for the New Zealand Countryside, A Planter's Guide by John and Bunny Mortimer originally published in New Zealand by Taitua Books in 1984"--T.p. verso.
Includes bibliographical references and index.
ISBN: 0-9632460-4-6 (pbk. : alk. paper)
1. Windbreaks, shelterbelts, etc.--New Zealand.
2. Windbreaks, shelterbelts, etc.--North America.
3. Tree planting--New Zealand.
4. Tree planting--North America.
5. Trees--New Zealand.
6. Trees--North America.
I. Mortimer, Bunny, 1923-
II. Title.
SD409.5.M672 1996
634.9'9--dc20   96-18694
                                                                      CIP

Manufactured in the United States of America
This book is reprinted on recycled paper.

Contents

Acknowledgments

Mrs. Rhoda McWhannell of Ohaupo really planted the seed of this book. It germinated and has been cultivated by us. With advice and help from those mentioned, it has grown into the specimen it now is. We are sure that if only a few more trees are planted as a result of its publication, Mrs. McWhannell will be very happy. We thank her for inspiring it and for her never-failing interest in its progress.

Diane Lucas contributed the chapter on Landscape Design. She is a landscape architect who was nurtured in the Central Otago high country. She took a science degree at Otago University and a post-graduate diploma in landscape architecture (Dip.L.A.) at Lincoln College before working for four years for the Ministry of Works and Development in Christchurch, Dunedin and the Hamilton districts. After overseas travel she returned to New Zealand overwhelmed by the beauty and diversity of the country but concerned at the tenuous understanding of rural landscape values and the complete lack of guidance available for farmers wishing to develop their land in line with these.

In 1979 she established a rural landscape practice based in Geraldine, South Canterbury and since then has worked mainly as a consultant to farming people. She is also active in developing greater public awareness of landscape values and has published a booklet "Landscape Guidelines for Rural South Canterbury" (1980-81), which is widely used.

Landscape designer Ines Stäger works with Diane and has been involved in the preparation of the drawings for this book.

The book has been written by lay people for lay people. Nevertheless a number of professional foresters and scientists have given us a great deal of help by checking drafts, offering research and assistance. In acknowledging and thanking members of the N.Z. Forest Service staff at the Forest Research Institute in Rotorua we must make it quite clear that they have had no formal input and can in no way be held responsible for any of its contents, nor do they necessarily agree with what has been written. In particular we acknowledge the invaluable help of the following individuals who helped make this book possible:

Ian Nicholas, Chris Ecroyd, Clive Anstey and Karen Nichols of the N.Z. Forest Service in Christchurch, Chris van Kraayenoord of the Ministry of Works and Development Soil Conservation Centre at Aokautere, Murray Faulkner, Dr. Ron Kilgour of Ruakura Agricultural Research Centre, Bob Berry of Tiniroto, John Mackay from Heriot, Ian McKean, David McNeil of Te Poi, Richard Davies-Colley (Past President of the N.Z. Farm Forestry Association), Bruce Treeby, the late Doug Revell, Tony Beveridge, and Dr. John Butcher. So many farm foresters have been called on for information and comment that we cannot mention them all. To all of you, thank you.

Foreword

It has long been my vision that a well managed landscape should look like a great green park, hence the name we've adopted for our book publishing division--Green Park Press. In a park, vistas open and close as you walk through it. Grass and trees intermingle and offer alternative choices of light or shade. I believe the hand of man and the hand of God are most in harmony in a mixed grass and trees park. I, like most people, believe a landscape gently and knowingly touched by man is far more beautiful than one left completely wild.

I first visited John and Bunny Mortimer's farm near Hamilton, New Zealand, several years ago. There, for the first time, I saw the green park I had carried in my mind for so many years actually existed. Carefully planned to be both beautiful and functional as an income-producing, mixed livestock/forestry property, their farm included such whimsical treatments as a stone circle and a hybrid Greek ruin just to add fun. Today, their small farm has been donated to the city of Hamilton as an arboretum and opened to the public.

When their book **Trees for the New Zealand Countryside** arrived as a gift from our New Zealand correspondent, Vaughan Jones, I knew I had to share its valuable ideas with my fellow North Americans. In our hemisphere, non-industrial forestry concepts are as hard to come by as snowballs in Mississippi. I have added some North American examples to their book to show their ideas work well in this hemisphere. Also, in adapting this book for use by North American readers, Editor's Notes, marked by [] within the text, and North American Notes have been added. The intent of this additional text is to further stimulate your thinking about integrating trees into your grass farm.

In the Southeastern states, cattle and timber were always integrated until the advent of corporate forestry. The thick barks of the fire-resistant pines offered excellent protection from grazing damage. Unfortunately, the piney woods grazier and the college educated corporate forester frequently suffered from a "crisis of communication." Neither understood the other's goals and problems. The management of two enterprises requires a higher level of management and a broader knowledge than monocultural management. Narrowly trained people will always try to simplify the world down to match their training. In most instances, the cows were banned from the woods. Today with both environmental and liability concerns over smoke from controlled woods burning, more and more foresters are becoming "cow friendly." In the Pacific Northwest, sheep graziers are actually being paid to graze Douglas Fir plantations for vegetation control.

In U.S. Forest Service research in Louisiana and Florida, it was found that intensively managed pasture in combination with extensively managed woods pasture provided the best livestock returns. Livestock research has long shown that a "put and take" grazing system offered the best harvest of intensively managed pasture. The question was always where do we "put" them after we "take" them. A good answer in pine tree country is "in the woods." However, combining grazing and forestry benefits the trees as well.

Managed grazing allows a wider tree spacing, which gives better tree growth and requires much less burning for the removal of understory vegetation. LSU's Professor Emeritus, Dr. Bill Oliver, wrote in the **Stockman Grass Farmer** that one could produce pine timber in the Southeast better with cows than without them. We may never go to hand-pruning trees as is done in New Zealand, but such management-intensive forestry options are very feasible on a farm-scale forestry operation.

I personally think a monoculture landscape of pines, peanuts, pumpkins or pasture is visually boring. Like the Mortimers, much of my vision has been shaped by the English landscape where great care is taken to soften the hand of man and make it blend in with its countryside. I think there is great value in planning the way a farm looks. Trees that soften the hard edges of buildings and barns have a value far greater than their sawtimber stump value. These landscape lessons are included in this book. The Mortimers pointed out to me that once a farmer starts planting trees he sends a signal to his neighbors that he is taking a longer view, and this will ultimately result in greater economic returns. No doubt a thoughtfully planned, integrated forest-pasture, green and growing landscape will add much more value long-term than the white board fences wealthy pastoralists currently use to signal their good fortune to others.

An Englishman once told me that the most productive pastures are always stolen from the forest. In other words, pastures and forests in humid environments exist in a state of dramatic tension. This means that with management, forestry and pastoral agriculture can be mixed and mingled so as to serve multiple purposes that complement each other. A pastoral farm can utilize and create value from the byproducts of its forestry enterprise better than any other type of farming enterprise. Some of these uses are firewood, fence posts, forage, bedding chips, shelter and shade. Just as the production of meat, milk and fiber should be a byproduct of farming pasture, the production of saw timber, veneer and plywood could be seen as a byproduct of producing shelter and shade in a management-intensive pastoral context.

As more and more North Americans see the beautiful landscape that a management-intensive, mixed forest/pastoral farm can produce, I am sure many will join me in my vision of turning our continent into a great, green park.

Allan Nation

Preface

"The planter of trees is a man of vision. He has the wisdom to realize that trees are needed for his physical comfort and his spiritual welfare. He knows that they are necessary for the well-being of his land and for the protection of his stock. Above all, he knows that trees are the vital heritage of the future."

These are the opening words of the preface to F.B. McWhannell's book **Eucalypts for New Zealand Farms, Parks and Gardens** published in 1958. They are entirely appropriate to any book which sets out to encourage tree planting, but especially so to this book since some of Mr. McWhannell's earlier writings have been used by us.

We do not set out to provide sufficient information to enable identification of tree species, rather we hope to identify the many purposes for which trees can be used. We want trees to be seen as part of the total landscape: they can not only improve production but can have a considerable impact on the quality of life for both people and the animals which provide them with a living.

So many farmers provide shelter around the homestead as a first priority but leave their livestock exposed to cold winds and hot sun. There are landowners who persist in trying to farm a piece of low-producing land when a well designed and managed woodlot would be better land use and a good form of diversification. Water is a crucial ingredient in production, and storage dams provide summer supplies for irrigation and drinking. At the time when the need is greatest, hot summer winds cause unnecessary evaporation losses, which could be reduced by planting trees on the windward side. We take for granted the vital role which bees play in pollinating our plants. We think hardly at all about the steady destruction of the very environment necessary for them to live and do their job. We should be planting trees to ensure that there is a constant food supply throughout the seasons. We can also make provision for bird food and habitats by planting suitable trees, for a world without birdsong would indeed be a sad place, probably filled with many more undesirable insects.

Because of our tendency to try and extract the last dollar, small wet spots are frequently drained to produce another few miserable blades of grass. So often greater benefit would be gained by planting moisture-loving trees, which can help dry out the area and provide wonderful autumn colors. The effects of erosion can be seen as our precious topsoil slips away, never to be replaced unless we provide a new forest cover to supply more humus and to hold the land together. Flat areas, too, are losing topsoil, and tree barriers can prevent a loss of tilled topsoil in times of high winds. The staple diet of our grazing animals is grass and clover-- almost as much a monoculture as some of our pine forests. Seasonal changes bring feeding shortages, which could be alleviat- ed by planting suitable forage trees. These not only provide food but bring benefits through the additional nutrients contained in the foliage, fruit and nuts.

If your home is near a factory or highway, planting of trees is a most effective acoustic barrier as well as a visual one. So many farms have iron sheds and white-painted water tanks, which would be the better for having a few trees to hide them from neighbors and passing motorists. Often such unsightly structures are hidden from the farm house, but the effect of them on the landscape generally (and therefore on other people) is overlooked.

Farmers and the many other people who make decisions affecting our countryside need to accept that they have a responsi- bility to the whole of the community, for the view from the road belongs to us all. History clearly tells the story of how our native forests have been destroyed (a process which unfortunately still continues in some areas). Original forest cover is replaced by a farming landscape which now has to be molded into not only a productive asset but also one which should make a positive contribution to our environment. Unless we preserve the small pockets of native trees which remain on our farms, and keep on planting trees (both indigenous and exotic) in accordance with good design principles our descendants will give us little thanks for what we have bequeathed them.

There is nothing difficult about planting trees--the rewards far outweigh the effort required to establish them, and once that is accomplished they continue to grow and contribute their many values with hardly any additional input by the landowner. There should be no conflict between production and tree growing; it should be the converse for there is an interaction between trees and most living things on the farm and these can be complementary. Landowners, those working on the land, city dwellers and the domesticated animals on whom we depend, all benefit both directly and indirectly from trees. The multiple land use concept, now so much more acceptable, has trees as essential ingredients. Let us acknowledge the diverse values and functions of trees and how greatly they contribute to our landscape values and to the environment of those who live and work in our rural areas.

"We should do our utmost to encourage the beautiful for the useful encourages itself." (Goethe)

Introduction

This book has been compiled to help those responsible for land management to make greater use of trees. The planter should think in terms of the effect that is required and then select the tree best suited to the site. Your local extension agent can suggest trees that will grow well in your locality. There is nothing more liable to failure in every way than a plant that is in an environment to which it has not adapted. Everyone likes to see a strong-growing healthy tree and this means avoiding planting in unfavorable sites or planting trees with susceptibility to insect damage and diseases. Unsuitable sites result in slow growth, defoliation and vulnerability to secondary infections--and the trees look awful.

As practicing farm foresters we have found that there is no publication which can serve as a handbook for larger landscape planting. There is plenty of information available in the many gardening and horticultural books, but only one has so far been published with the farmer in mind. This is George Stockley's **Trees Farms and the New Zealand Landscape** published in New Zealand by the Northern Southland Farm Forestry Association, which has been a source of reference and information in the writing of this book. We have confined our subject to trees, a term which generally does not cover anything likely to be less than 23 feet (7 meters) high when mature. In our experience no single book supplies all the answers and it is frequently necessary to refer to several to get the information one seeks.

We have been very involved in tree planting ourselves and this has led to our acting in an advisory capacity to other farmers. Visiting their farms and discussing their objectives, we have so often been at a loss to leave them something which would continue to act as a guide after the specific recommendations which we have made are carried out.

Shelter

Interest in shelter is now so great that a chapter finally had to be included and we are most grateful to Murray Faulkner of Centrepoint Nurseries for supplying a first draft and to Ian Nicholas of the NZ Forest Service for helping to edit it. On its own it is a subject to fill a book. Our contribution sets out some useful guidelines.

Shade

Shade and its effect on animals and pasture seem to be a somewhat neglected subject. There is practically no scientific literature based on New Zealand research and little that we could find based even on observation or interest. When we see how animals use shade and how we ourselves appreciate its availability, it seems worthwhile including some aspects of its effect on livestock.

Planting Design

We start the book off with the design section by Diane Lucas because we would rather nothing was planted until this has been read, if not completely digested. The community has the right to ask of the land owner that he or she take into account the effects his or her actions will have on the surrounding countryside. More intensive land use and a steadily growing population occupying small holdings are rapidly changing the view from the road, mostly for the worse. Our vistas are framed by power and telephone poles and lines: a plethora of galvanized unpainted iron sheds spoils the country, situated as they often are close to the road on the 4 hectare or 10 acre farmlet or on the skyline of the larger farm.

On a visit to England during the course of preparing this book, we were, as are most travellers, overwhelmed by the beauty of that country. On analysis it appeared that most of the pleasing aspect was manmade--if one can include under that heading the planting of trees. Only very rarely were power or telephone lines seen. New Zealand's reputation for beauty depends almost entirely on its natural physical characteristics--the mountains, the rivers, the forests and the coastlines. The cultivated parts of the country are becoming less beautiful as civilization imposes its ugly additions. In England there are stringent regulations on what can and cannot be done to the environment, and while it is a landscape planner's paradise, it is a nightmare to anyone wanting to put a building up in a rural area. The result however is a satisfying and comfortable blend of agriculture and buildings, with neither shouting at the other. It is a unified, harmonic scene, and with the work being carried out by the Countryside Commission, England has a charm all of its own and remains one of the world's most beautiful countries.

Stand on a hill overlooking an urban area and note the "spotty" effect of white houses and silver sheds. Do the same in England and you will see the mellowness of buildings of brick and stone, the natural materials of the area and in harmony with the landscape. Can we not learn from this and have a care for our rural scene? We hope that the design chapter will assist you in planning your farm so that it becomes more attractive from every point of view, making it a more pleasant environment to work in, more satisfying to those who just look at it and maybe adding capital value to it as well.

We do however recognize that putting into practice a planting scheme in accordance with the best design principles as set out in Chapter 1 is not easy. There are many areas of conflict and planters will have to work out their own priorities. We anticipate farmers and foresters disagreeing with what has been written, but no apology is required. It is important that the approach to planning be made with the ideal in mind, although almost inevitably compromises will be necessary. If only a proportion of the objectives are achieved, then the landscape will still look the better for them.

Climate

Exposure is generally the main difficulty in establishing trees in coastal areas, but there is plenty of wind inland too. Altitude differences add to problems, so in this book we have tried not to be too specific as to where a tree will or will not grow. Microclimates will produce variations in survival and growth.

Remember that whatever the statistics might say there is always the likelihood of unseasonable weather conditions, the late frost being the one most likely to do damage.

The change to metrics has meant that we in New Zealand can no longer use degrees of frost as an indication of severity of cold. The book mentions frost, but generally describes tolerance to cold in terms of degrees Celsius. For those who still think in terms of Fahrenheit these Celsius equivalents may be of some assistance:

$$1° \text{ frost} = -0.6°C$$
$$5° \text{ frost} = -2.8°C$$
$$10° \text{ frost} = -5.6°C$$
$$15° \text{ frost} = -8.3°C$$
$$20° \text{ frost} = -11.1°C$$

Frost effects can be minimized by ensuring that there is adequate air drainage. Cold air gets as close to the ground as possible and then rolls downhill if there is no physical barrier. If frost is an inhibiting factor in tree establishment make sure you leave an escape hole for it to go through. If you have protectors such as old drums, leave a gap at the bottom for air drainage (both cold and hot). Young trees which are slightly frost tender should be hardened off before planting out. Don't take them straight from a protected nursery area, exposing them to a temperature which they have not experienced. Gradually move them out into the colder areas so that if they should be subjected to late frosts after planting they are less likely to suffer. Autumn frosts can damage soft tissues, so if they are expected a scrim cover can help. Late spring frosts are unpredictable and you have to take your chance. Careful site choice and pre-planting treatment will help to minimize damage. Eventually trees will grow above frost damage so protection may be required for only a year or two.

Choice of Species

This is a book about trees, so you will not find any detailed description of species which do not normally grow to at least 23 feet (7 meters) at maturity. Smaller trees are mentioned in the specialized areas such as shelterbelts where they may have a specific role to play.

Work with your local extension agent who can suggest fast and slow growing trees that are indigenous to your area.

Fruit Trees

Most farmers agree that livestock thrive on grass and clover. They resent the presence of weeds, and some regard trees as unnecessary, whether for shade, shelter or supplementary fodder. Others believe trees encourage diseases through stock "camping" under them. But many think that feeding animals on deep-rooting plants such as certain "weeds" and trees provides stock with minerals which are not found in the top few centimeters of soil occupied by surface-rooting plants. Trees recycle these minerals by the dropping of their leaves which, if not eaten by animals (or even if they are) return their elements to the topsoil as they decompose.

Timber Uses

To produce quality timber nearly all trees require some training and form pruning. Ideally the bole should be free of side branches for 20 feet (6 meters)--this distance being related to the size of plywood which is normally processed into sheets. A log pruned to 20 feet (6 meters) allows a little wastage at top and bottom and can then be veneered into suitable sizes. This length is also acceptable from a miller's point of view, should the log be destined to produce clearwood.

The expression "of no commercial value" is sometimes used. This means that the timber is not normally in demand by the marketplace and would be difficult to sell. It does not mean that it is worthless--we have found that almost all the trees mentioned in this book are widely used in their country of origin and have many intrinsic qualities. It is usually the size of the resource that puts a value on timber. The marketplace has to be able to rely on continuity of supply if millers, manufacturers and retailers are to be equipped to handle the wood and the finished products. It is for this reason that the New Zealand Forest Service has formulated a policy advocating plantings of a limited number of species other than *Pinus radiata* to supply future requirements of special purpose timbers.

"No commercial value" may mean you cannot sell your tree to the local miller, but you may well be able to have it milled on your own account and use it at home. This may be for the farm, for firewood or to meet the needs of a woodwork hobby. You could even sell off the surplus to neighbors or the local woodcarver. The section on wood properties may help in deciding whether it is worthwhile making the effort to convert an unwanted tree into something useful.

We emphasize here that planters must look around their own neighborhood to see how species perform. Inquire from those who have achieved success with their trees. Don't be diffident about knocking on the door of a farmhouse where there is evidence of successful establishment. Keen tree-growers are almost invariably delighted to help others interested in doing some planting by passing on the stories of their successes and failures.

1: Planting Design

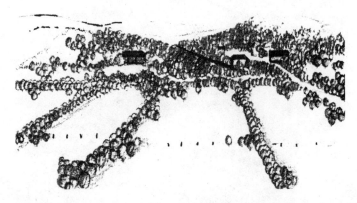

Productive open spaces within a productive wooded countryside.

Much of the countryside is dominated by arbitrary, formal patterns defined by property boundaries, roads, fences, and plantings. These straight lines and grid patterns would mostly disappear if the rural land were left unworked and ungrazed, for trees and shrubs are the natural cover for most of the country. Natural patterns would reappear, patterns which relate to the underlying land form, with its variety of soil, moisture availability, aspect and microclimate. The landform or topography pattern is the basic component of any landscape, and is emphasized by vegetation. Even in a functional farming landscape the topographic pattern can still be emphasized by vegetation. By planting to show the variations in topography, soils and climate, local character for every different area of the country can be developed. Emphasis on **natural** variety should be a priority, otherwise the whole of a country would look the same.

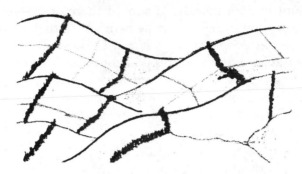

Countryside dominated by formal, arbitrary patterns...

...and the patterns that would develop naturally.

Although variety is important, it is not desirable to have random mixtures of exotic trees spread haphazardly about the country with no relationship to the locality. Exotic, ornamental mixtures can be very destructive of local character. Care is needed in species choice and siting to ensure that all plantings will look as though they belong and are not imposed "unsympathetically". Plan all plantings as components of a pattern of open and wooded landscape. The shapes of the plantings, and the openings, need to be closely related to the shapes of the underlying landform. The size of the spaces will depend primarily on the intensity of the land use, particularly in relation to the amount of shelter required: systems of productive open spaces within a productive wooded countryside.

A landscape that displays a sense of naturalism is universally preferred to that which is obviously man-dominated. The principal aim in planting layout should therefore be to do away with, or soften, any straight lines. Remember too that the landscape does not stop at property boundaries. Design your plantings to emphasize the landform features that continue from one property to another (e.g. ridges, valleys, waterways). Discuss plans with your neighbors to ensure that you work to complement one another and enhance the local character in this way.

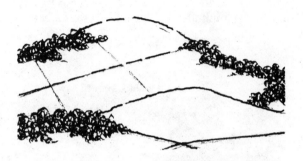

Planting that relates to topography.

In designing farm planting, care is needed to avoid destroying the beauty that already exists. Before planting any tree or tree mass, consider the relationship with the surroundings. Generally a tree should not be a prominent feature in complete contrast to the surroundings. Instead, the scale, color, shape, and texture should be in sympathy with the landforms and with other vegetation. Formal plantings and arrangements are often unsatisfactory because of individual failures and growth rate variations. Also, formality usually conflicts with landform patterns. It is very difficult to develop a formal planting that really looks right, as the scale of the planting is critical in relation to the spaces. If formality is wanted, it is best achieved within an informal framework, but of course the transition from formal to informal needs to be carefully designed.

Because of their small size, shrubs and small ornamental trees look too fussy for the rural landscape. They belong in town gardens, or within larger tree frameworks of rural gardens. To use shrubs and small trees successfully in the rural landscape they must be massed together so that none appears as an individual specimen.

In the choice of species make maximum use of local vegetation, using local native species which are particularly adapted to the conditions, and exotics that grow well in your area. Even "weed" species of trees and shrubs can be useful. Take note of what is growing well already. A design with many healthy trees, even if a limited number of species, will be more successful than a design that uses a wide variety of trees, some of which struggle under the conditions.

Trees should also meet visual requirements for framing views and screening, enclosing spaces, integrating structures with their surroundings and enhancing local character. Each planting should fulfill as many functions as possible while aiming at maximum beauty in the landscape. Multi-purpose plantings can be achieved by using a mixture of species, with each species having one or more function. A single species can be used to meet a number of needs, but for ecological and visual reasons it is not desirable to have very extensive single species plantings.

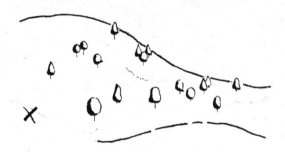

Mass trees together so that none appears as an individual specimen.

Local Character

The visual character of a landscape is influenced by the topography, the existing scale, type and pattern of vegetation and land use, and the prevailing color of rock, soil, and structures. This character determines not only the extent, types, and patterns of planting that will look right, but also the appropriate siting, forms, materials and colors for patterns and structures.

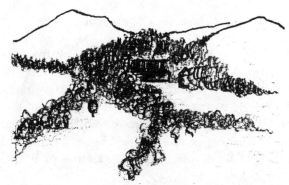

Buildings can nestle into a planting network.

Local character can only be enhanced by recognizing the natural diversity of the landscape through maximum use of local native plants mixed with useful exotics or alone. If these plantings are designed in relation to the landform, a suitable and logical landscape character can be developed.

Framework Planting

Each farm planting, whether for shelter, timber, shade, screening or beauty, needs to be designed as part of a framework which reflects the patterns of the natural landscape and visually absorbs the various rural developments. Buildings and silos can be nestled into a planting network so that these structures become an acceptable part of the landscape. Existing vegetation including shrubland remnants, riverside willows and woodlots can be used as a basis. Extend these with plantings for shelter, etc., but always in a pattern which follows the topography.

Special tree groups fitted into the network.

If particular ornamental trees are wanted they must be fitted into this framework and not be set apart as isolated elements or decoration. Groups and groves of special tree species should serve some functional purpose: screening, shade, fruit or nut crops, valuable timber, or to highlight particular soils or microclimates. There should not be an obvious contrast between trees for use and trees for decoration. All planting should do both--be beautiful and useful.

Trees and Climate

Trees change the microclimate for people, animals and other plants.

Temperature

Trees make the climate milder. Within trees temperatures are modified, so it is cooler on a hot day, and frosts are rare.

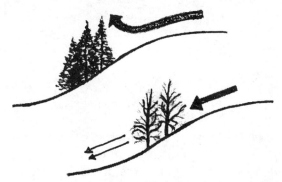

Dense planting across a slope can dam cold air, increasing frosts. Cold air is heavier than warm air, so it slowly flows off hills into valleys, collecting in frost hollows. Even flatter ridge tops and plateaus can have pools of cold air, so that these sites can experience frosts almost as severe as valley sites. The upper slopes of the valleys have the least frost--the thermal belt. [See illustration next page.] Maximize such sites for planting and living, as in all districts of the Northern Hemisphere the upper South-facing slopes will have the highest minimum temperatures.

The main damage from frost occurs when the sun reaches frozen plants. By planting in shaded areas (shaded at least from morning sun) the plants will thaw slowly so that damage is less likely. Plants in bare ground are less likely to frost than those in mulch.

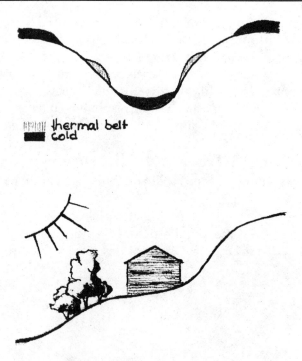

thermal belt
cold

Maximize the warmer sites.

Dense plantings such as shelterbelts reduce winds and may dam cold air so that temperatures are colder at night. But during the day soil and air temperatures in the sheltered areas are significantly higher. Dense shelter plantings can be sited above and shaped to deflect the cold air away from critical sites.

Moisture

Trees also modify moisture levels. Because of shade and shelter the soil under trees usually dries out less, depending on whether trees are shallow rooting or not. As much of North America's rain comes from the North and West, the Southern sunny sides of plantings will be drier than the rain-catching sides. The dry Southern side that is sheltered from rain is the 'rain shadow' area.

rain shadow

Moisture limitations may decide the minimum spacing of trees: trees need to be wider spaced in drier areas, and closer in moister sites. Weed control and mulching significantly reduce watering needs.

Too much moisture is a major limiting factor for tree growth. Tree species which tolerate "wet feet" can be used to reduce excess soil moisture, and less tolerant tree species (or crops) can then be interplanted. For this technique to be effective, winter-growing evergreen species are necessary. Trees can also be used instead of a drainage system to lower the water table through high rates of evapo-transpiration, but this should be done sparingly. It is not necessarily desirable to drain or dry out wetland areas whether by tree planting or earthworks and thus cause a loss of landscape and ecological diversity.

Deep-rooting trees tap moisture and nutrients and supply these as stock fodder in times of drought when shallow-rooting species (e.g. grass) are under stress.

Lush growth gives a visual key, even when surface water is not visible.

Tree species that naturally grow alongside streams can often be used to enhance valley and waterside character. For example, willow, poplar, and alder are associated with lush sites, so their appearance gives a visual key to the site even when the water is not visible. But take care to avoid destroying natural plant and animal habitats alongside water, and to avoid the trees spreading where not wanted. Dull, fine, dry-looking plants (such as pines, eucalypts, and acacias) convey a dryland character, signalling higher or drier sites. The change in plant character from watercourse to upland slope visibly reinforces the landform pattern.

In tree crops too, the soil moisture can be displayed in crop choice, with juicy crops generally on the lusher lowlands, and dry crops (such as carob) on dry hillsides. The presence of irrigation can be boldly displayed by integrating the lusher trees in shelter and crop plantings, and along border dikes.

Sunlight

It is critical to supply enough shade to avoid concentration of stock under just a few trees (see the chapter on Shade). Scatter trees and tree groups around paddocks to ensure adequate summer shade. The trees can extend from shelterbelts or woodlots to soften the layout; they can be grouped strategically to frame good views, screen bad views, produce a nut or fruit crop (walnut, chestnut), produce special timber (oak, ash, beech, poplar), and create interest in the landscape.

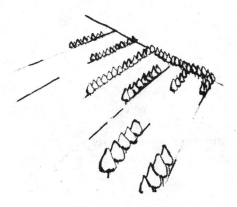

Trees can extend from shelterbelts to soften the landscape.

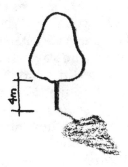

Deciduous trees with clear trunks at least 4 meters (13 ft) high provide good stock shade. The shade is projected away from the tree's base and moves around during the day. The stock move with the shadow so that their camping is not concentrated in one place. Winter shade is minimal.

Late-leafing deciduous trees can be used where maximum winter and spring sunshine is needed on crops, etc. Align shelter plantings North-South wherever possible to obtain maximum sunshine on the area between the groves or rows of shelter plantings.

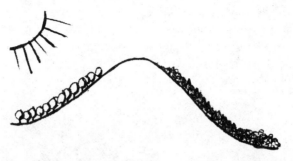

Edges of plantings and slopes, which face South in the Northern Hemisphere, receive maximum solar radiation. They can be used for trees and tree crops which require greatest heat and light (most fruits, Honey Locusts). Likewise sites shaded by topography or trees can be used for trees which prefer or tolerate such sites (hazel, most conifers).

Wind

Wind is a major limitation to tree growth. Without wind, moisture stress is markedly reduced. Shelter planting can be a major use of trees, but care in design and management of these plantings is essential to avoid the trees causing other problems.

The subtleties of rural landscapes must be especially respected in shelter design. As shelter planting often forms the basic framework of a farm landscape, it must be carefully planned with more than just shelter in mind. Too often the shelterbelts carve up a landscape with formal plantings that destroy the local character. Shelter design should not automatically involve the laying of a grid over the farm. Study the natural shelter created by the topography and vegetation and develop a shelter planting design around the landform patterns as an extension of this natural shelter.

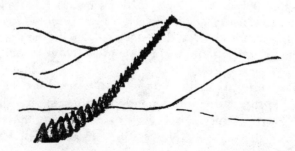

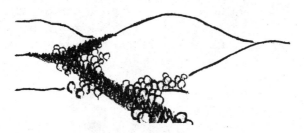

Shelter planting related to the topography.

An existing fencing layout should not automatically be used as the shelter layout pattern. Fences and gateways not sympathetic to the landform need to be left unplanted, or be resited. Nor does shelter necessarily need to be in the form of straight rows of trees.

In pastoral situations it may be preferable to use irregular groves and clumps of trees scattered about to diffuse and lift the winds. (Land uses such as cropping may limit the suitability of scattered tree clumps.)

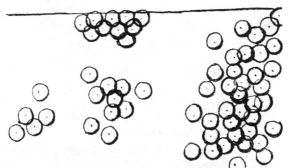

Tree clumps to diffuse the winds.

Not only are there visual problems with long rows of trees, but if the shelterbelt does not lie at right angles to the path of the wind, then the wind can be accelerated along the belt. If the long row is broken by a gap for a gateway or power lines, this gap will become a wind funnel.

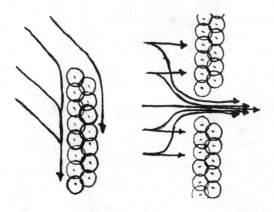

Where rows of windbreak planting are required, always try to run them **with** the lines of the land--the valleys, terraces, swales, waterways, soil boundaries, etc. A layout that does not relate to the landform will soon dominate the landscape. Permeable windbreaks of rounded form and soft color will disrupt the landscape less than windbreaks of dark, dense, formal trees. Generally, broad-leaved trees are less disruptive than conifers.

A straight-row shelterbelt should not suddenly start or stop. Each belt needs to be linked with other plantings, having a wider end group, and continue some way in another direction. If only lineal plantings are used, considerable care is needed with their siting as any straight line or geometric shape will become a dominant element. In rolling or hilly country if the siting, form, or color of a shelterbelt is not sympathetic to the landform, or is isolated and not tied into a general landscape framework, it can visually destroy a far greater area than the actual farm.

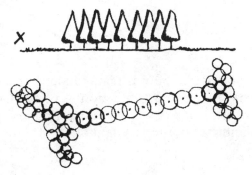

Avoid abrupt, straight shelterbelts.

Developing shelter plantings from local native vegetation would help a lot to produce distinctive local character. These plantings could also be valuable for creating a network of wildlife habitat, and for providing bee fodder. Fussy, garden-style, ornamental trees and shrubs should not be added to shelterbelts as they do not suit the farm-scale landscape. Mix species informally in all plantings: never alternate different kinds.

Use shelter planting to emphasize the landform pattern:
 ● Where shallow valleys lie across the path of the wind, the valley system can be emphasized and good shelter provided by planting along the drainage pattern line. Not exposed ridges, but valley floors or lower slopes are better sites for tree growth. Tall trees in the valley bottom will give shelter to adjoining ridges.

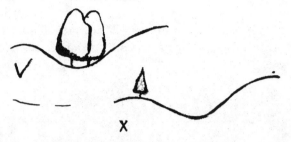

Even if a single or double row is planted along the watercourse, make it less formal by widening into groups, particularly at change points--on the outside of a curve; up into a tributary; extending to form shelter plantings running at right angles to the valley.

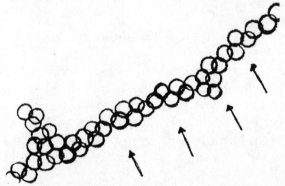

Shelter plantings running along a valley.

Native water-side tree and shrub species added to exotic trees, or used alone, will give considerable character and interest. Take care not to encroach on the riparian zone with inappropriate plantings. Protect buffer zones between productive land and waterways; protect any remnant or regenerating native vegetation, especially that surrounds a spring.

● Valleys which are wind funnels will require planting across them. To retain the continuity of the valley landform, use shelter trees of open form and soft green color. Use lush-looking species, possibly deciduous.

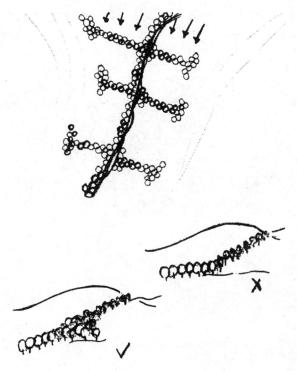

If the belts are required to extend up the sides of the valley, there should be a gradual change in tree species to relate to the change in landform. But employ a similar soft shape, e.g. poplars on valley floor, eucalypts and acacias on drier valley sides. Soften the change from one to the other with group plantings of a mixture of each as a small woodlot, two-tier, or corner copse. Sudden changes and sharp contrasts should be avoided.

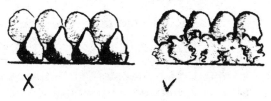

Add lower, denser shelter to the high, permeable trees only if absolutely necessary, such as for critical stock or crop shelter. Any density immediately cuts the visual landscape flow (and could collect cold air). Soft form and color in the lower story is essential-- never use conifers.

If an understory is needed, use a mixture of local native trees and shrubs, possibly adding some multi-use plants such as fruiting, bee and stock fodder trees and shrubs.

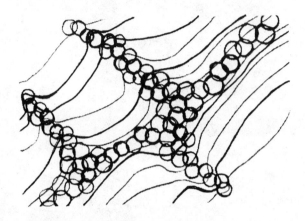

Ensure any shelterbelts that cross a valley are strongly linked into more dominant plantings along the waterway. Cross shelterbelts should appear as extensions from this central spine.

● Hills and ridges suffer considerably from wind exposure, so they are the most difficult places on which to grow shelter trees. The higher and steeper they are in comparison with surrounding landforms, the more important they will be in the landscape. Skylines will be the most prominent sites. Because of this visual prominence, as well as the adverse conditions (wind exposure, moisture extremes), any hill planting needs to be carefully designed if it is not to become a blot on the landscape. Generally, rounded tree forms which are not very much darker than the surrounding landscape are preferable.

No shelterbelt should go straight up and over a hill or ridge. If it is necessary to run a belt over a ridge, then ensure the species vary with the different sites. Try to avoid planting the ridge-top areas. Often trees do not do well in such a situation, yet will be visible for many miles around. Subtly link the shelterbelts into woodlots, gully plantings, and those extending up from the valley, so that no shelter is a lone strip across a slope.

Soften the appearance of all straight-line plantings by extending them to fit the contour of the land. Wherever there is room, an awkward corner, or a change in slope or moisture, widen the planting to form substantial groups, possibly extending some trees out into the paddock to give a more gradual transition to pasture.

Visual contrasts between rows should be minimal. For example, if there is a contrast in color, say slightly lighter and darker greens, then they should be of similar form and texture. Generally it is preferable to contrast just one aspect--either form, or texture, or color. With formal shelter-planting layouts, contrasts in two or more aspects look unhappily contrived.

If conifers must be used for one or more rows of a shelterbelt, an informal mixture of different conifer species will lessen the starkness of the belt.

Formality will be reduced by adding groups of broad-leaved trees but avoid any stark contrasts between the different species. Only slight variety within the rows is desirable. If conifers are used, then an informal mixture of two or more different species which have similar growth rates will be preferable to a row of one species. The same applies to broad-leaved trees.

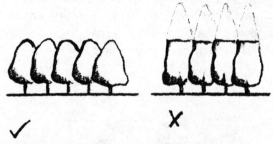

Relatively even tree height is desirable for effective shelter. But avoid topping or hedging trees. Instead, plant trees that will grow to the desired height.

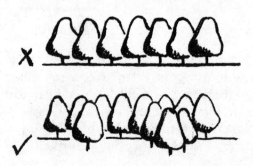

Sometimes only a single row of shelter trees is required, such as for an intermediate planting to subdivide between major windbreaks. To improve the visual depth and balance, add further trees to widen the row at some points. As with widening out any shelterbelt, these extra groups should show some relation to the landform and help create more interesting spaces within the farmland.

In planning the layout and design of shelter be sure to work with the existing landscape, complementing the landform patterns and the natural shelter. Take care to protect and encourage any remnants of native forest and shrubland that do remain.

Woodlot Design

Developing a woodlot which is a beautiful feature of the landscape does not mean adding a few ornamental trees around the edges of a standard block of pines! There are wonderful opportunities on so many farms to develop small, interesting woodlots of special-purpose timber trees. Hill and valley farms are often particularly suited to varied woodlot development.

The actual productive forestry planting must be carefully sited and designed to complement the local landscape. If it is not, instead of an asset the woodlot can become an ugly blot on the landscape.

The location, shape and extent of forestry plantings are critical. Forestry can add to the beauty of a landscape by adding interest and variety that looks logical and sensitive. Or, as too often happens, forestry can totally ruin it with insensitive plantings which obliterate or dominate natural beauty and character.

Forestry planting should not be considered in isolation, but must be developed as part of a total plan. Aim for best land use, multiple use, and coordination of all plantings into an overall framework that complements the natural landscape.

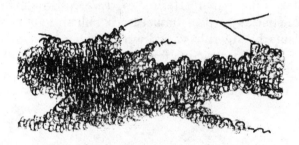

Carefully protect any remnant native forest or shrubland that you have by fencing out completely with no gates. Retain the bush for local identity, interest, wildlife values, and to protect soil and water resources. It is distressing to see a distinctive vegetation being cleared to be replaced with a monoculture of timber plantings which do nothing for development of local identity and which could be anywhere. The need is to build local character, not to destroy it.

Instead of trying to clear, spray or burn areas of shrubland to develop pasture in areas that will require high maintenance input or place soil stability at risk, use the shrubland as the first stage in the development of forest. Either allow or encourage native regeneration, or interplant with native and/or compatible timber trees. It is a waste of resources to continually clear shrubland on land that is obviously better suited for tree growth.

There is a need for high-quality timber trees to be grown, and these require soils of reasonable quality. The planting of small, special-purpose woodlots on good soils could be very beneficial: such land use diversity gives variety in work opportunity and products and at the same time adds to each property's beauty.

In the siting and design of a woodlot, take care with:

1. Relating the woodlot to the landform pattern.

● Fit the overall shape of the woodlot to the topography. The steeper or more visible the land, the more care is needed with designing the shape.

● Relate the outline to natural boundaries. Never follow geometric boundaries, nor have the edge of a woodlot running straight across or up a slope. Avoid sharp-angled edges on a hillside. Do not automatically follow fence lines or property boundaries.

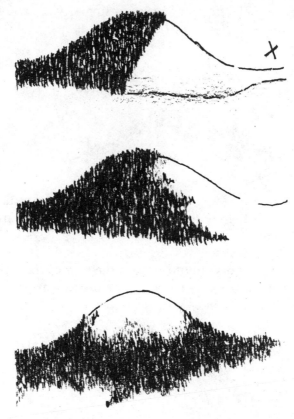

2. Avoiding skyline planting.

● The boundary between land and sky is a very important landscape feature. Take care not to disrupt this boundary. Never suddenly start or stop a plantation on a skyline--a careful transition is essential.

Preferred forestry on any ridge or hill top is hardwoods for long-term selective logging. These are usually of softer form and color than conifers. The selective logging does not have the devastating visual effects of clear-cutting. Avoid short-rotation, clear-cut forestry systems on ridges and hilltops.

3. If trees must be in rows, have the rows running around the hillside with the contour. Do not have rows running up and down a hillside.

4. Mixing species.

● All woodlots should have a mixture of tree species. The only exceptions are small woodlots of broad-leaved trees (oaks, blackwoods, walnuts, etc.), which can be beautiful as pure stands.

● A continuous plantation disguises the underlying details of the landscape. Therefore it is important to mix species in such a way as to display the details rather than disguise them. Change species where there is a change in soil, aspect, moisture or slope.

● Plant long-rotation hardwoods to give a framework when the other species are felled. This framework should follow the main pattern of the landform--the waterways particularly, suitable spurs and ridge lines, and parts of the outer margins of the plantation.

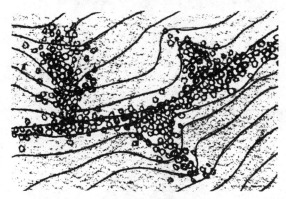

It does not need to be continuous, and should not be of constant width, but vary informally, widening out into groves at strategic points and narrowing to nothing at others.

● Do not have sudden changes from a block of one species to a block of another. Mix the species where they meet, merging one type into the other. A guideline for the amount of mixing required for a plantation containing two species is to have a third to a quarter of the area in a mixture of the two species, the remaining two-thirds to three-quarters being pure stands of each species.

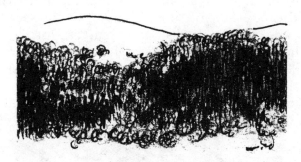

● Temporary plantation mixtures such as a nurse crop and the species it protects can be quite ugly. Alternate rows of contrasting trees should not be visible, and never run up a hillside.

If two different types must be closely mixed to produce both a nurse crop and a long-term crop, plant them in mixed groups, not in long rows.

5. Treatment of edges.
● Avoid straight, sharp edges. Those of a woodlot need to be softened to create a pleasant transition from forest to pasture. Do not plant a narrow fringe of ornamental trees around the edge.

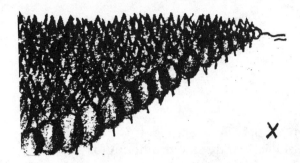

Instead:

  • Plant large groups and groves of other productive trees, and have them drift back into the main crop. The drifts should relate to the landform pattern--run up gullies, ridges, or terraces.

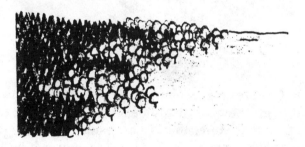

  • Have the plantation trees wider spaced toward the edges. Create a gradual transition from dense plantation to grassland. Distribute the trees irregularly--not in rows.

Even though the main plantation may be high-pruned for timber production, reduce the amount of pruning toward the edges, so that the transition trees have a balanced shape. The transition trees will also be more wind-firm, and may be capable of remaining when the main crop is harvested.

X

6. Forest-farming combined.

Although there are many benefits from closely combining timber trees and pasture, the visual results can be ugly. Never plant wide-spread rows of trees across rolling or hilly land. The effect is very dominating. Wide-spaced trees are beautiful when combined with pasture if they are grouped. The forest-farming concept is very successful where the trees are carefully sited in an informal arrangement, which meets the needs of both industries.

Using multiples of five as a pattern basis for planting layout.

Trees and Buildings

Most structures in the countryside appear as an intrusion: they often look as though they have just been dropped there. There is no sense of belonging, either in their siting or their design.

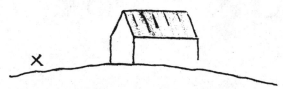

Although it is desirable that all structures be of dull, earthy colors--with walls at least as dark as the surrounding landscape, and roofs much darker--it is not always practical to paint existing large sheds. Nonetheless no building should sit stark and shiny in the landscape. If a building cannot be suitably colored, then use trees to screen and soften the structure. Even two or three trees can be a great help.

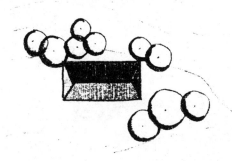

All buildings should be sited so that they have a backdrop, preferably of land as well as of trees. Nestle structures against existing vegetation wherever possible, and supplement with additional planting where necessary. The backdrop planting should be tall enough to appear well above the roof, but need not be planted close to the building.

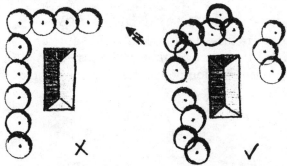

     X   ✓

Trees forming a backdrop or screen should not be planted as a row around a structure. It is not usually necessary to block out a building completely, but merely to reduce its impact. Group trees so as to integrate the structure subtly into the surroundings. Tall trees should be sited around the North side of buildings. These trees can be a deciduous and evergreen mixture, with the latter being an understory to give good low shelter. They can be as much as 50 to 80 feet (15 to 25 meters) back from the building, although they can often be much closer. It is visually important that the planting is extended around the ends of buildings, softening their outline and thus relating them better to the surrounding land.

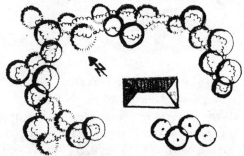

Plant tall, deciduous trees on the South side of buildings. These will make a building look more interesting, as glimpses are always more exciting than total exposure. At the building, these South-side trees will give some shelter, summer shade, privacy and beauty. Views out may be possible under the tree canopy.

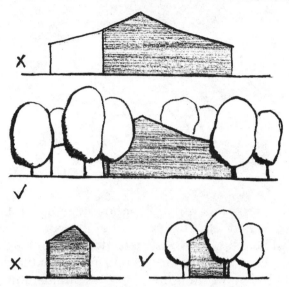

Many new farm buildings look so enormous that their apparent size needs to be reduced by planting trees to break up the form. Such planting must be tall enough to extend well above roof height. Awkward building forms can be improved by using trees to direct attention away from the form. The trees soften the angles and edges and create a more appropriate silhouette to relate the building to the surrounding landscape. Buildings of completely different style or scale should not be visible in the same view. Screen-plant with trees so that only the one style is visible from any viewpoint.

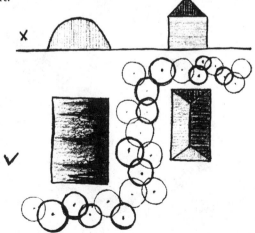

Plant trees to link various buildings together and coordinate the scattered variety of structures that appear on so many farms. Breaking a silhouette is more effective than camouflaging it with creepers, etc. It is not necessary to screen a structure completely; merely soften it by planting to break the outline and reduce its impact.

Composition

Informal layouts are more likely to look good than formal ones.

Formal Design

To plant formally--in straight rows at even spacings--is a major decision to take, because the formality will dominate the character of any site. Take care never to use formal patterns which contradict the natural patterns. The steeper a site, the more dominating and inappropriate formal planting will look. For a formal design to be successful, the proportions must be carefully related to the size of the space. Too often formal plantings are too small to frame an area adequately; they are out of scale.

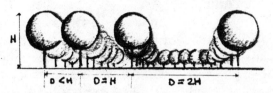

A space can be pleasantly enclosed by planting if the width of the space is no greater than a distance twice the height of the enclosing trees. Wide spaces cannot be comfortably enclosed by small trees.

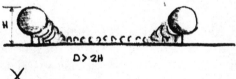

If trees are placed in a row at regular spacings, they must grow evenly or there will be visual conflict. Formal layouts are often not successful because of individual tree failures, or variations in growth rates. If one tree fails, the pattern will be upset. To ensure even growth rates, it is necessary to use just one kind of tree in a formal design. A mixture of species can never create the essential unity.

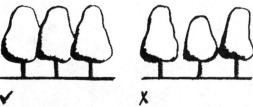

Simplicity is critical for a formal planting to succeed. Use just one kind of tree, and plant them close enough so that their branches intertwine by the time they are half grown. A design dependent on trees of a mature size can look unsatisfactory for many years.

As planting should reinforce the natural patterns of the landscape, formal layouts are very rarely suitable except on totally flat and uninteresting topography. Even on an apparently flat site, planting can be used to emphasize natural patterns to make it more interesting and more logical.

Informal Design

Planting layouts which are informal are more likely to complement the landscape, especially where they emphasize the natural patterns. Informal does not mean haphazard. Plan informal plantings involving subtly controlled compositions which appear more natural than contrived. Alternatively, allow the trees to sort out a completely natural pattern through natural regeneration; seeding; or mass planting of seedlings where survival is greatest in the best sites, thinning out toward less favorable areas, thus giving natural transitions.

Have a look at plants that have colonized naturally-- whether native trees or shrubs, or weeds--observing the spacings between the plants, from dense to sparse in relation to the site conditions. Use this type of grouping in planting design.

Mixtures of different tree species need to be treated in the same way, with dense groupings of one kind thinning out as another kind mixes in, and gradually merging into a dense group of the second kind. The groupings should always vary in size. This basic design technique can be applied equally to drifts of trees in the paddocks or along drives and to mixing plantation species as well as in the more controlled situation of narrow shelter planting.

Basic Principles for Grouping Plants

Using trees, shrubs or even herbaceous material, to achieve a balanced composition that may be viewed from any angle:

1. Do not place one tree on its own. It would be too vulnerable and usually appear out of scale at least for the first few decades. A group is far more likely to be successful and each tree does not need to be a perfect shape.

2. If only two trees are to be planted, then they must be of the same kind and should be planted so close together as to appear to be growing out of the one hole. They should appear almost as one tree with their branches intertwining.

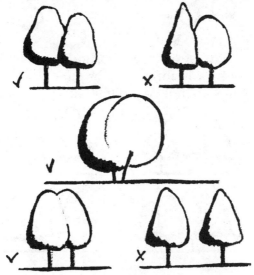

3. Vary the spacings between trees.

● A group of three trees should have two close together so that their branches intertwine, and the third slightly further away.

● For a group of five, have three close together, a fourth just slightly further away and a fifth further away still to appear as a transition out from the main group.

● For groups of seven or eight or more, increase the spacing from the center outward.

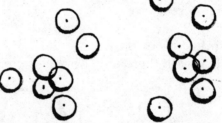

4. Do not have strongly contrasting trees within a group. If there is to be contrast in form, then be sure that the scale, habit, colors, and textures are not very different.

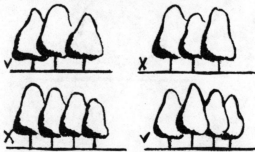

5. Have the tallest-growing tree(s) near the center of the group. Do not step heights from tallest to shortest, but step up to near the center of the group, and down again. Do not step up and down symmetrically.

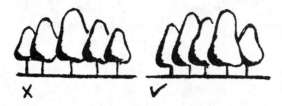

6. Where deciduous and evergreen trees are to be included in the same group, have evergreen species mainly towards the center. The greatest density should be in the middle of a group. Therefore to ensure the group appears balanced in winter, keep the open deciduous trees to the outside of any evergreens.

7. Where both broadleaf (hardwood) and conifer (softwood) species are to be included in the same group, generally keep the conifers toward the center. Conifers are usually more formal and dense than broad-leaved trees. The broad-leaved trees need to be placed on the outside of the group to soften and "round down" the overall form of the group.

8. Mix trees within groups:

● In a group of three trees, have them all the same type, perhaps varying only in size through planting trees of different ages.

● With a group of four, have all of one type; or one of a larger growing species, and three of a slightly smaller type.

● In a group of five, have all of one type; or three of one type and two of another.

● For a group of seven, have all of one type; or four of one type and three of another.

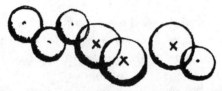

● A group of 10 trees is the minimum size for having as many as three different species within a group. A group of 10 trees can be beautiful if all are of the one type;

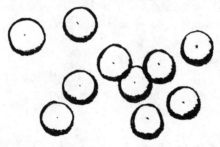

or a mixture of 2 species--perhaps 7 of one type and 3 of another, or 5 and 5, or 6 and 4;

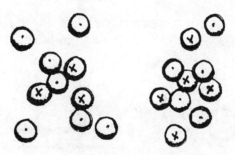

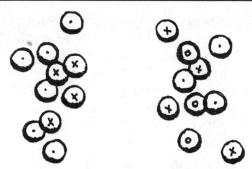

but three different types could be used in a group of 10 trees--4 of one type, and 3 of each of the other two types.

9. Any group of trees should not be a separate composition, but should link into the surroundings--relating to the landform patterns, land use patterns, and to other vegetation.

Each group of trees should relate to any other planting nearby, mainly by repeating some of the same trees, or at least trees of very similar scale, form, texture and color.

10. Where several tree groups are planted, continue at least one type from a group into the next group. This visually links the groups to give some essential unity.

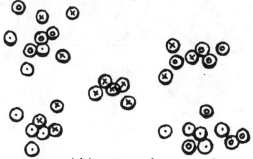

11. Group trees within rows: plant trees in rows only where absolutely essential due to limited space. Grouping can reduce the formality within rows. Never alternate species.

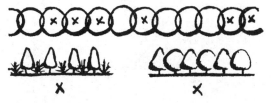

When mixing, use species that do not contrast too much. Vary the form, or the texture, or the color to a slightly deeper or lighter green. Greater variation is warranted if conifers must be included in the row. Because of their stronger form it is generally desirable to include a subtle mixture of conifers and also add broad-leaved trees to soften them. As in all groupings, it is important to "round down" the edges. Broad-leaves informally added to a conifer row will achieve this effect.

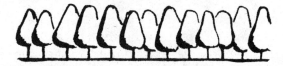

Vary rows of trees by planting a few extra trees, of the same kind, outside the line, especially toward the ends of rows. Where two or more rows stand side by side, either mix the species throughout, so that contrasting lines do not result, or group trees at the end to screen this view.

12. If trees are massed together with shrubs underneath greater variety is acceptable. Trees and shrubs of contrasting form, habit and texture can be grouped and mixed; if closely planted to mass and intertwine. A considerable variety of local and native species can be informally massed to enhance local character.

13. Mixing species: Whenever different tree types are mixed, make sure the contrasts between the types are subtle. Each type of tree has a particular character which can be defined in terms of its form, habit, texture and colors. These qualities need to be carefully studied to assess the visual compatibility of various tree types.

Form

Look at the overall shapes of different trees broadly categorized as round, conical, columnar, horizontal, or weeping.

Observe which nestle into a landscape, and which create accent points. The round forms nestle into most landscapes and are most likely to complement landforms. Grouping different round tree forms together usually creates a very restful planting.

Conical trees can be appropriate. With their height much greater than the width, they emphasize the vertical scale. With the wide base they appear well anchored in the landscape. Groups of just one species of conical tree, or mixtures of several conical types, can look very effective. But unless the conical trees are leafy and soft-looking (generally broad-leaves rather than conifers), it is often preferable to use them as accent trees within a group. Have round form trees towards the outside.

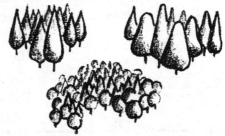

The more extreme forms such as columnar, weeping and horizontal, are very difficult to integrate. They are dominating forms, and thus are best avoided. The columnar form of the Lombardy Poplar has become part of the distinctive character of some districts. Occasionally it may be desirable to continue this character down within a valley. If this strong columnar form of the poplar is to be used, several should be placed centrally in a group, with tall rounded trees grouped around to soften their forms. Lombardy Poplars should neither be placed in a row nor in a group on their own.

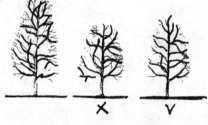

Do not alter the form of a tree by pruning, topping or other mutilation--it is preferable to let it grow into its natural state. If tree surgery is required, be sure to carefully retain the natural form and habit of the tree.

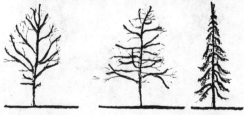

Habit

As well as the form of trees, the habit must be carefully considered when deciding which species are visually compatible. Habit, the branching structure, provides the character of the tree within its total form. Trees generally have either ascending, horizontal or descending (weeping) branching patterns.

In addition, the strength and detail within the branching pattern give individual character to a tree species, e.g. the rugged, elbowed branches of the White Oak; the fine pendulous branches of the birch; and the sweep of sequoia branches.

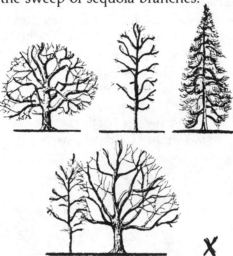

It is important to have only subtle contrasts in habit within any tree group. Never group strongly contrasting habits together-- not dainty pendulous with strong vertical. Within a group, habits should be of similar boldness, even if the branching is in differing directions.

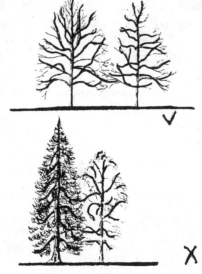

A strong vertical and a strong horizontal may be quite acceptable together, but a dainty horizontal and a strong, angular horizontal may conflict. For example, although a European Weeping Birch (*Betula pendula*) is basically of descending form, and the Giant Sequoia (*Sequoiadendron giganteum*) has branches sweeping downwards, they should not be used together as the birch is very dainty whereas the sequoia is very strong.

Group trees of similar habit for a restful, pleasing composition. Although some contrast can be included for accent, this must be carefully controlled to avoid conflict and chaos.

For many tree species the form and habit vary at different ages, perhaps from a pyramidal form with ascending branches when young, to a rounded (or almost square) mature form with horizontal to descending habit.

Texture

In addition to the overall form and habit, each tree has a pattern formed by the leaves and twigs. The play of light and shade on leaves and twigs creates the pattern, or texture.

Texture results from the size and spacing of leaves and twigs; the shape and division of leaves; surface quality of leaves (smooth or wrinkled, shiny or dull); and the length and stiffness of petioles (leaf stalks). These qualities together give either a coarse, medium or fine texture which is significant from both near and distant views.

A coarse texture results from large leaves (e.g. Sycamore) and will be more coarse when the leaves are widely spaced giving shadows between the leaves (e.g. Catalpa). Small leaves give a fine texture. With cut leaves they appear finer (e.g. Honey Locust, Mimosa-tree or Silk-tree). Coarse, strongly textured trees (e.g. Horse Chestnut, Catalpa) create focal points, and must be carefully sited. Dense, medium-to-dark colored foliage which is not so coarsely textured is well-suited as background or general framework planting (e.g. Red Oak).

The density of the foliage is important. Fine foliage can be set so close together that instead of appearing fine and delicate the tree appears heavy and solid. Dense coarse foliage has the appearance of strength. Short stiff petioles emphasize this strength.

In planting design, aim for subtle contrasts in texture. Use stronger contrasts if the trees are very similar in other ways--similar in size, form, habit, and color. Or the contrasts could be related to time--the texture of a tree can vary between the seasons, and with age.

Color

All farm planting should look as though it really belongs to the landscape. To achieve this, summer-green foliage is essential. In recent years, planting for dramatic contrast has been so overdone that garish mixtures have resulted. Contrasts in foliage color have destroyed the beauty and restfulness of many landscapes.

There are a number of reasons for completely avoiding non-green foliage forms in any planting design. Pale cream, variegated, and golden foliage is so much lighter and brighter than the usual green foliage. It visually dominates other green vegetation, attracting attention away from the subtle contrasts within and between plants.

Seasonal change and interest are important in any landscape. The changes in foliage, flowers and fruits allow different plants to demand more attention and become more dominant at various times of the year. But this happens only during their display of flowers, fruits or autumn foliage.

Variegated and golden forms can also give the impression of being unhealthy. They do not have the fresh appeal of green foliage. For these reasons it is considered advisable that all golden or variegated trees be completely avoided. Removal of existing ones is usually necessary. Foliage which is red, purple or russet in summer can also be very distracting--it appears almost as autumn color in the wrong season. Generally avoid such colored trees.

Although colored forms may have initial appeal for many people, usually this wanes as they come to appreciate the subtle visual values of plants. Contrasts in texture, in the different tones of green, and particularly the changes with the lighting and the seasons, provide so much interest they can really be appreciated only if there are no variegated or colored foliage forms in view. The garishness of the latter overpowers the subtleties of the former.

For the same reason that colored foliage is undesirable, so too with bright flowers and fruits that completely cover a tree. Bright flowering trees, such as pink flowering cherries, and bright fruits, should be kept in the garden, not out in farmland views. If they must be used, ensure there is an ample background of rich green foliage all around. Strongly colored stems of deciduous trees (e.g. red, orange, yellow) usually appear too strong for the rural landscape in winter.

If for some reason colored foliage is required (for floral art, specialist horticulture, etc.) then such plants need to be grown within an enclosed space where they can only be viewed close by. They should never be part of the general scene.

2: Trees, Pasture and Soil

Agroforestry may be a new word, but the concept of mixing pasture and trees goes back to when the first crops were sown by primitive man (in those unenlightened days the work was usually done by women). Since he tended to destroy the forest to make room for cropping, it was more by accident than design that some trees survived. Older civilizations soon learned that food-bearing trees could be grown as a complementary crop. They also learned much later that land going through the cycle of forest, field and plow often finished up as a desert, as the removal of topsoil by wind and rain became inevitable. The world is full of such disaster areas and in spite of the knowledge available to us now, there are many examples of flatland agriculture practices being applied to steep hill country. It may not be through cropping, but the effect of forest removal and heavy stocking has resulted in enormous quantities of precious topsoil being lost.

Studies in New Zealand included measurements of pasture production over a period of three years on land which had been heavily eroded in the past. They showed that after three years, pasture growth on scars was about 80% down, on average, compared with uneroded ground. Even after 50 years the pasture growth on old regrassed scars was about 23% down, on average. By integrating the proportionate areas of eroded ground with the reductions in pasture growth, the loss in "potential productivity" was obtained. Results to date showed that the overall loss in potential pasture growth of these hill slopes was 16% on average. Further work is expected to show that this figure is somewhat optimistic, i.e. the reduction may be more serious than this. This figure could increase significantly with future erosion events.

Trees are natural crops for steep lands for they can store water much better than grasses; their deep-rooting system also seeks out moisture well below the surface. They can withstand drought much more effectively, but above all, the trees' widespreading roots hold the land together. Crop-bearing trees are a permanent agriculture so we should be looking much more closely at this form of land use: trees holding together topsoil, which continues to grow pasture on which livestock can be grazed.

We tended in the past to grow a forest as a first objective and then to use it for what grazing could be eked out from under it; not primarily for the benefit of the animals and their owners, but more to keep the forest floor clean, with easier access to trees, less fire risk and quicker breakdown of pruning and thinning slash. (Plus of course some useful income for the forest owner.) Recent thinking has been directed to a managed form of trees and pasture whereby the two become fully integrated and given equal status in the planned objectives. Side benefits are shade and shelter. The indications are that chestnuts, walnuts, pecans, persimmons and suchlike could play a worthwhile role in land use economy. An oak tree produces acorns by the sackful, Honey Locust can produce beans with a dry weight of over 2.5 tons per annum to the hectare (2.47 acres) off about 120 trees. Willows can produce 15 tons of edible dry matter per hectare (2.47 acres) per annum and some of the stock can continue to graze under these fodder trees. They are some of the permanent trees of agroforestry, but there is also a place for timber trees grown on a rotation basis.

Over the years a few venturesome farmers have put stock among their pine trees from a very early age. Perhaps even more farmers have seen stock among their newly planted trees as a complete surprise! There are many factors which affect the behavior of stock towards trees, some of them being most unpredictable. Livestock are capable of being managed in such a way that pine trees are not at risk even when quite small. This is particularly so when the same cattle are constantly exposed to pine needles, right from the time they are calves; similarly with sheep. Stock tend to damage trees more in the spring, when they have an urge to find some roughage not present in pasture, but bark stripping can often be attributed to different social and behavioral patterns. What needs stressing is that the management of two-tier farming has to be of a very high caliber. The dedicated stockman will give preference to his animals, the forester to his trees.

Compromise decisions will often be required, and the seekers of the best of both worlds may have disappointments.

Much has been written on the subject and a 30-year trial on fertile farmland at Tikitere, near Rotorua, is still in progress. After the first 20 years the summary of findings is as follows:

- Successful integration of farming and forestry requires clear objectives and a high standard of management.
- Trees grow faster on farms than on comparable forest sites.
- A high standard of silviculture is essential to produce high value sawlogs.
- In New Zealand, the large diameters on trees at low stocking rates do not compensate for the loss of volume for having fewer trees and the related loss of height.
- Tree quality findings show that both stem and branch size increase with lower tree stockings and generally wood density is lower.
- Pasture is adversely affected with clover and ryegrass decreasing and inferior grasses moving in. In highly stocked areas of 400 stems per hectare (170 per acre), substantial areas are smothered by pine needles, pruning and thinning slash.
- Nutrient status, apart from nitrogen, indicated all elements were at adequate to high levels. There has been a slight drop in pH. No earthworms are left.
- Livestock performance is little affected by trees up to 100 stems/ha (40 stems/acre). Above 200 stems/ha (80 stems/acre), performance declines. There is no evidence to suggest that lambing percentages or meat quality are affected by understory grazing.
- Decisions on tree stocking rates are directly influenced by the landowner's perception of relative farm gate prices for agricultural products and forest products.

Dairy farmers having high-value land are usually reluctant to use grazing pasture for trees. However, by planting timber belts along fence lines, it is possible to grow a tree crop. Electric fencing protects the trees from the cattle. There needs to be not less than 40 m (131 ft) between belts. To maximize sunlight it is best for them to run North-South. It is essential that trees be regularly pruned to at least 6 m (20 ft) to avoid side branching and shade.

A New Zealand trial on a heavily fertilized farm now milking 400 cows has shown that there has been no reduction in milk solids production over 10 years--in fact, it has increased as cow numbers and quality have grown. (Effective area farmed has increased by 50%, cow numbers by 100%, and milk fats by 148%.)

After 12 years there are now the equivalent of 36 acres of *Pinus radiata* woodlot planted at 644 trees per mile (400 trees per kilometer) at 8 ft (2.5 m) spacing. This is forecast to produce 3000 cubic yards per mile (1400 cubic meters per kilometer) of merchantable logs at age 26--by which time shading will have reduced pasture growth, but after clear felling, one can start all over again.

This book is no place to try and cover the subject in any depth, although much of its content is sympathetic to the philosophy of multiple land use, incorporating the concept that trees and farming are complementary, not competitive. To ensure that all the options for land use are fully considered, agroforestry should now be incorporated in all management planning and decision-making.

The loss of topsoil is such that protection forestry is vital to retain what is still left, but the opportunity for forest grazing is still there. Widespread planting on marginal country appears to be a viable prospect if the demanding silvicultural regimes can be adhered to. Evidence from the New Zealand Radiata Task Force is that the best economic returns are obtained from large logs which are produced from early thinned plantations, or wide spaced plantings of trees, particularly those possessing superior genetic qualities. While the main thrust of research is on radiata pine, other species respond well to such regimes. For instance poplars are very happy growing in isolation from one another. They can produce fine quality veneer logs, they can help to dry out a wet spot, the grass grows right up to their trunks, their prunings provide edible stock fodder, they give summer shade, color up well in the autumn and then allow sunlight onto winter pastures. On steeper country they do all this and as well control land movement.

In the summer of 1978 there was a serious drought in the Wairarapa of New Zealand. Former National President of the Farm Forestry Association in New Zealand, Jim Pottinger, was desperately short of food on his Tinui farm. After weaning calves at the end of July, for two months he fed his nearly 200 mixed age in-calf beef cows on a diet of poplar leaves, small twigs and branches. Nothing else: young stock had already taken all the grass. The total area used was 45 hectares (111 acres). These trees are still doing their original job of controlling erosion and providing shade and beauty with potential as a timber crop.

Wide spaced planting can be carried out with almost any of the timber or nut- or fruit-bearing trees, but if high quality logs are wanted then systematic pruning is absolutely essential.

Agroforestry is just another form of diversification which enables farmers to maximize the production of the land in line with its particular qualities, and potential, and the skills and wishes of the owner. It need not take up much space. A few Black Walnuts on a choice site will hardly be noticed and yet in 50 years each one could yield a couple of cubic meters of timber--and could be worth the equivalent of about 10 finished steers. There will be no loss of productivity, yet a few small stands of high-quality trees will certainly add to the value of the farm.

Because research is rapidly making new information available, this form of diversification should be carried out only after doing lots of homework and seeking out the best advice and latest techniques likely to give the best results. This will benefit not only the farmer, but the whole landscape and so the community will be the final beneficiaries. And what is wrong with that?

Loss of topsoil should be the concern of every landowner, but especially those who are making a living from their land. They have a responsibility to think in the long term, but unfortunately most do not give much thought beyond 20 years. Even when it comes to tree growing we have been conditioned to the 25-year rotation of Monterey Pine (*Pinus radiata*). Erosion is a severe and extensive problem. Both prevention and repair are needed to ensure that rates of soil loss are held to or below those which took place before development. This can be achieved by adopting wise land-use policies; only then can we look to productivity being maintained for centuries rather than decades. Good land management must include preservation of the resource, and the wise use of trees is a management option open to all landowners.

A Few Thoughtful Tree Tips

● Poplars are just one tree species that can be used to prevent hillsides slumping. Cattle can enjoy poplar prunings in hot, dry weather.

- High-pruned poplars provide shade for animals and will make good veneer logs.
- A high yielding Honey Locust will produce more than 100 kg (220 lbs) of beans each year.
- Pines, poplars and sheep can all grow well together.

North American Notes:
Pine Trees and Beef Cattle in the South

The integration of beef cattle and pine timber production has existed in the South for over 300 years. Traditionally this was a rangeland type of operation utilizing a small-frame, early maturing, very thrifty type of cattle. The average stocking rate for this type of operation was 25 to 30 acres per cow, which wasn't bad in the open range days when it was largely free feed.

Today, there is no free open range in the South. While woodland range grazing is still a viable and profitable option on very large properties, pine timber and cattle co-production can be greatly increased with intensive management.

Research at the Hill Farm Research Station in Homer, Louisiana, in the late 1980s found the following:

As much high value, clearwood saw-timber could be produced at 100 trees per acre as at 300 trees per acre.

When pine trees were stocked at less than 200 trees per acre, as much forage was grown under the trees as could be grown in open pastures without pine trees.

The forage to support a cow and a calf for the spring, summer and fall could be supplied by 1.25 acres of bermudagrass/tree pasture fertilized with 100 lbs of nitrogen per year.

Dr. Bill Oliver, LSU Professor Emeritus, summed up this research by saying, "Cattle production can be as good, and timber production can be better, when forage and timber are grown together on the same land."

- If cultivating high quality hardwood timber is your goal, wait until the terminal leaders of the trees are out of reach before stocking grazers/browsers in your woodlots.
- John and Bunny Mortimer have found that dairy cattle are much more abusive of trees than beef cattle. They have had no problems with beef cattle damaging grown trees.
- Research conducted in Oregon and British Columbia on young plantations of Douglas Fir and Lodgepole Pine showed that

cattle and sheep selected the new growth of seedlings almost exclusively during a narrow window of time in the spring immediately following bud break. Apparently, at that time, succulence of the needles, from the animal's point of view, was at its highest peak. As the season progressed into summer and fir and pine needles matured and hardened, animals progressively paid more attention to herbaceous vegetation. The stock were closely monitored, but were never held in an area so tightly that they were not able to select from among several forage and browse entrees.

• Researchers in the Pacific Northwest have found that livestock were much more effective than herbicides in controlling unwanted vegetation in pine plantations. Also, they noted that the livestock actually made money rather than costing money like the herbicides.

• Hardwood tree trimmings if chipped and spread on the pasture are worth about $10 a ton in fertilizer value. However, wood chips when used first as a source of bedding and then composted before applying to the pasture can realize a net benefit of 30 to 50 cents per cow per day.

• Sawing your trees into lumber will increase their value by a factor of three to five times over the stump sale price. The value added by a sawmill is one of the highest in manufacturing. Portable bandsaw mills can be purchased for as little as $8000.

• Tree bark makes the best material for surfacing dairy walk-back lanes (raceways) in that it is dust-free during dry times of the year. Tree bark is often free at pole-peeling plants.

• Always cut stumps close enough to the ground to allow a tractor and rotary mower to safely run over them.

• Dragging the cut top of a tree over a freshly logged area will create enough soil surface disturbance to enable grass seeds to germinate.

• Slash Pine (*Pinus elliottii*) is favored over Loblolly (*Pinus taeda*) in the Gulf Coast region for integrated tree-pastures because of its early rapid growth and open crown. Tree spacings of 6 x 16 or 8 x 12 feet (1.8 x 4.8 meters or 2.4 x 3.6 meters) are best. If closer spacings are used, at least every third row should be wide enough for truck passage to haul away fence post and pulpwood thinnings produced in the early years of growth.

- In Florida research, a 4 X 8 X 40 feet (1.2 X 2.4 X 12.2 meters) spacing of pines appears to be producing as much timber per acre as the traditional 8 X 12 feet (2.4 x 3.6 meters) spacing. This wide spacing allows the planting of winter annuals for dairy or stocker cattle.

- Research has shown that tree growth is stimulated by pasture fertilization. However, heavy use of nitrogen fertilizer can create insect problems and cause young pine trees to bend and warp, thereby ruining them for high value uses.

- Pine trees should always be planted in the winter just before newly sown grass seed. Newly sown stands of grass do not affect tree survival, whereas old grass stands can cause severe soil moisture problems in the summer. When planting pine species other than Loblolly and Slash into mature pasture stands, a 12 to 18 inches (30-45 centimeters) plowed or herbicided band may be necessary.

- Before planting a particular species of tree, review its past history of insect and disease problems in your area with your state forester's office. If the risk of loss is great for a given tree species, consider alternate sites or species.

- Bluestem woodland range in the Southeast will produce yearling gains in excess of two pounds a day from mid-March until May 1. Conversely, unsupplemented animals can lose up to 200 pounds on the same range in the fall and winter.

- Planted pine plantations in Louisiana naturally lend themselves to subclover planting because of the absence of hardwoods, and even, wide tree spacing. Initial plantings should only be undertaken during adequate fall soil moisture levels.

- Subclover can be established in existing tree stands if all hardwoods are removed. Trees are thinned from 75 to 80 trees per acre and a summer burning regime is established. Subclover appears to offer Southern livestock producers the promise of a very high-quality, low-cost, cool-season pasture.

(Authors' Note: Many New Zealanders believe that burning destroys the productivity of the soil by removal of the vital humus.)

3: Shelter

During winter months feed requirements are reduced
when there is good shelter.

The importance of shelter has been well demonstrated over
recent years by the expansion of successful crops such as kiwi fruit.
The sheep farmer also knows the benefits of protected areas during
times of lambing and late shearing. Unexpected gale winds and
even light zephyrs can cause stock losses which are often considered acts of God when in fact they could have been avoided
through proper use of shelterbelts.

Damage to export-quality horticultural crops, and stock
deaths, are obvious results of insufficient shelter, but the insidious
wind effect on crop growth and yield is much more difficult to
quantify. Plant growth processes are a complicated matter,
although most growers understand the necessary balance of light,
moisture and temperature. Transpiration (water usage) losses from

a plant are greatly reduced when wind speeds are lowered. This has a double advantage of ensuring that leaf stomata remain open (enabling photosynthesis to continue with the potential for increased yield) and that the plant is warmer, which increases the rate of photosynthesis. High rates of transpiration caused by the wind will accentuate drought stress.

There is little information on the response of grasslands to shelter despite their importance to world agriculture. Nevertheless in a review of world literature, J.E. Radcliffe shows that yields from tree-sheltered areas are increased by percentages ranging from 15 to 100 and more. The author emphasizes the need for grassland shelter research to quantify the benefits which are known to be provided by shelter. Uncompleted research trials indicate that increases in dry matter yield at distances of 3-5 times shelter height compared with 12 times are very substantial--accumulated pasture growth tdm/ha were 5.51 at 3 times the height, 5.40 at 5 times the height, only 3.28 at 12 times the height from a mature shelterbelt. Many farmers in windy situations are convinced of the effectiveness of shelter on grassland production. On stony, drought-prone soils in mid-Canterbury, P.W. Smail estimated that 20% of his farm production was directly related to his tree planting, and the total area of trees occupies only 5.6% of the property. This does not include the residual value of the trees, which when well grown and managed can provide both shelter and quality timber.

A 1981 trial under actual farming conditions gave dramatic crop increases on a Methven, Canterbury farm in New Zealand. The crop of oats was partially protected from hot dry Northwest winds by a single-row shelterbelt of Douglas Fir 1804 feet (550 meters) long and a mean height of 23 feet (7 meters). The belt had been side trimmed twice and was reasonably permeable. The worth of the shelter in economic yield was very evident at full crop maturity. The yield from the sheltered area averaged 35% increase over the average from the unprotected area with the maximum of 51% coming from crops situated at 4 times shelter height. Yields from 1 to 6 times the shelter height were significantly greater than a distance of 10 to 30 times the shelter height.

Apart from the wind's effect on the productivity of a crop, there are many other undesirable results that can occur under exposed conditions. It is perhaps more positive to summarize the benefits of shelter.

- Reduces mechanical damage to foliage, flowers and fruit, thus increasing crop yields.
- Reduces severe burning from salt-laden winds.
- Improves market value by ensuring better fruit quality.
- Encourages flight of pollinating insects and so improves fruit setting.
- Limits staking of trees to prevent root damage.
- Reduces topsoil erosion and protects newly seeded crops.
- Reduces crop flattening (e.g. hay) and seed loss.
- Protects stock, especially newborn animals.
- Improves stock comfort and reduces animal heat stress in summer.
- Reduces feed requirements during the winter months.
- Controls snow drifting.
- Creates a warmer working environment in winter.
- Improves the microclimate, thus widening the range of land use options.
- Improves spraying conditions, thus minimizing drift.
- Promotes straight trunks in timber trees.

In almost all exposed situations the farmer plants shelter around the house knowing that family and pets will appreciate the benefits and that the garden will be the better for the improved environment; yet more often than not the same farmer is reluctant to plant shelter over the rest of the farm.

Good shelter can minimize spray drift.

Extracts from some Australian reports on the benefits of shelter are worth quoting in full:

"Previous research in Armidale (Australia) has shown that vertical shelter increased plant and animal production on adjacent areas....Present experiments have confirmed the increase in plant growth and suggest that the growth is not achieved by increased growth per day when there is adequate moisture, but by availability of moisture for a longer period in the sheltered areas. Increased animal production results from the greater plant production.

"Significant differences in water use and evaporation were noted between sheltered and unsheltered plots. Green plant availability is generally higher in sheltered paddocks--about 30% at a stocking rate of 10 sheep/ha (4 to the acre), and with shelter regeneration of pasture is faster.

"The effect of shelter with varying stocking rate shows:

"At 10 sheep/ha (4 to the acre) liveweight gains were higher in paddocks without shelter. At 30 sheep/ha (12 per acre) there was little difference.

"At intermediate stocking rates the sheep with shelter were up to 16% heavier.

"At all stocking rates more wool was grown by sheep in sheltered paddocks."

There is growing awareness among farmers and orchardists of the benefits of planting trees that can supplement the nectar and pollen sources, particularly during the spring period when nectar and pollen production are low. Some shelter timber species are favored by the bees, such as *Eucalyptus, Acacia, Robinia, Gleditsia*, etc. Shelter provides a favorable working environment for the bee, increasing its activity as well as encouraging the growth and flower production on the pollen and nectar-bearing plants. Bees hate wind.

Principles of Shelter

The invisible flow of wind has very similar properties to water where the fluid takes the line of least resistance; flow rates and turbulence are largely determined by surface irregularities of the area passed over.

There are four main contributing factors relating to effectiveness of shelter:

height, porosity, length and uniformity.

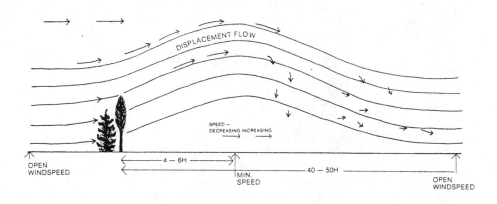

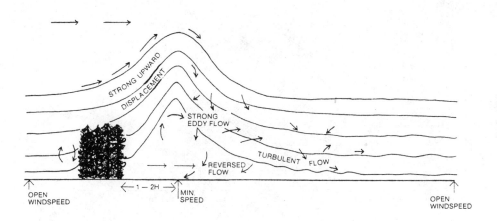

Diagrammatic representation of wind flow through
a permeable barrier (top)
and an impermeable barrier (bottom).

Height of the shelter directly influences the area of wind reduction on the leeward and windward side. The greater the height the greater the area influenced. Generally, good wind shelter is provided for 10 with some effect up to 20 times the shelter height on the leeward side and up to 5 times on the windward side; where a high degree of protection is required, e.g. some horticultural crops, belts are repeated at a factor of about 8 times the shelter height.

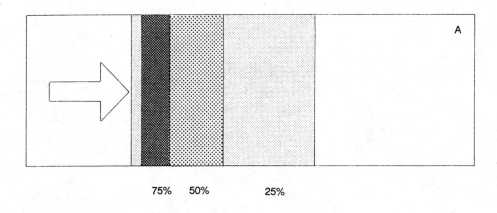

75%   50%   25%

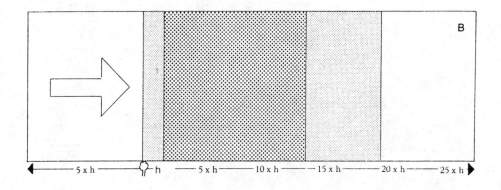

| 5 x h | h | 5 x h | 10 x h | 15 x h | 20 x h | 25 x h |

Distribution of zones of shelter at ground level, expressed as a percentage reduction of the wind velocity in the open. h--sheltered height. A--zones of shelter for belts of maximum density throughout their height. B--zones of shelter for belts of medium density throughout their height.

Porosity of the shelterbelt determines the wind behavior on the leeward side and to a lesser extent on the windward side. Practical experience has shown clearly that belts of medium porosity (40-60%) produce a much more even wind flow over a much wider area. Good porosity can be achieved by correct species choice and subsequent management. When porosity is low, the wind profile is changed; a very sheltered area occurs close to the belt but turbulence occurs at a factor of about 5 times the shelter height. An important advantage of live shelter as compared with artificial is that the leaves on the natural shelter respond to changing wind velocities, opening up as the speed increases, thus retaining the filtered air flow through rather than over the top.

A minimum length of about 20 to 25 times the ultimate height of the shelterbelt is desirable in order to maintain protection when the wind veers away from right angles to the belt, or when velocities are high, to avoid high wind movement around the ends of a short belt.

Gaps in a shelterbelt cause the wind to funnel through at excessive speed. This can happen where there are missing trees or when there is a draughty space at ground level. It is for this reason that a high standard of establishment and management is required; because of the very nature of the wind patterns through the gaps it is extremely difficult to fill them in later. Any early failure must be replaced as soon as possible.

To summarize, the ideal shelter can be considered as a tall narrow belt of trees with a wind permeability of about 50%, relatively uniform in height, no gaps and consisting of fast-growing, stable, disease-resistant trees with a reasonable life span. However many factors must be considered before such a belt can be obtained as each belt must be matched to the particular site requirements.

Planning

Because there are distinctly different needs from region to region and even within regions, shelter may require very special design and species choice to be effective. In planning future shelterbelts it is critical to decide what land use protection is intended. For example, a different degree of intensity in shelter establishment is required between arable farming and horticulture. Have a detailed look at what grows well in your area--visit old homesteads, talk to local landowners (farmers and orchardists) and to agricultural and forestry advisers and nurserymen. You will then learn what shelter designs have proved most suitable, and the various alternative tree species which have adapted well to local climate and soils.

The layout and planning of shelterbelts is an important exercise initially for the whole block. Future land use based on soil and topography will determine the intensity of shelter establishment and will highlight any constraints on choices. Once you have decided land use then planning requires decisions on orientation of belts, site problems, species choice, stock ordering, fencing and how much financial investment is needed.

Orientation. To maximize sun on both sides of the belt it should run in a North-South direction, so some compromise will often be required to achieve the best wind protection without harmful crop shading. Deciduous species should be considered for East-West belts to allow penetration of winter sun. Poor siting of belts can produce very wasteful land use--losses in production due to shading, competition to the crop and frost pockets--resulting in lower crop productivity. In general, existing fences will be along major ridges or drains and so cost of refencing may be a factor in the choice of shelterbelt location. Belts, where possible, should be aesthetically pleasing, and so compromises in some situations (e.g. near homestead blocks) may be necessary between having ideal shelter or retaining views--shelter should harmonize with the existing features of the landscape. Planting along natural watercourses (careful of species choice) can produce a very attractive landscape blending with the natural topography. (See Planting Design.)

Site Constraints: Having decided where the belts are to be established it is necessary to check on site peculiarities that will influence belt design, species choice and future management. Such features are proximity to buildings, overhead wires, landscape value, severity of exposure and proximity to salt-laden winds, natural fertility levels, presence of compacted subsoils, and natural soil drainage levels. All these constraints require noting before selecting the most suitable species and establishment methods required.

Species Choice: Knowing the objectives for the shelter and the site constraints it would seem an easy task to select the ideal tree species. The best choice can be considered as:
- Cheap to establish and manage.
- Fast-growing without excessive root spread.
- Maintaining desired height and density.
- Having a compact habit and being wind-firm.
- Requiring minimum maintenance.

● Provide resting sites for birds that feed on undesirable insects and bugs.

● Not harboring pests and diseases.

● Providing nectar and pollen for bees.

● And possibly the production of high quality timber, or animal fodder.

Most of the current choices available meet only a few of the above requirements. Therefore a certain level of management, e.g. pruning and trimming to maintain porosity, has to be carried out.

The disease risk associated with planting only one or two species has been highlighted by the effects of the poplar rusts discovered in 1973. The planting of several different species on the same property is now common practice in many areas. Given a range of trees suitable for shelter, every individual will choose differently according to his or her personal interests whether they be timber, bees, aesthetics, or wildlife habitats. There is no one choice but there is a choice for everyone's needs.

Ordering: When the species has been selected and quantities calculated it is sensible to order shelter and any other required trees well in advance of the planting season. By ordering at least six months ahead stocks will be assured, and your local nurseryman will be able to plan his stock movements too. This will ensure that good seedlings and service are available. Buying off the shelf at the last minute can be a disaster both in availability and quality.

Fencing: There can be no short cut to fencing out areas to plant and this requires careful organizing before shelter establishment. Stock proofing is essential to uniformity since once tree tops are eaten out, trees are severely set back, and subsequent growth is uneven and trees malformed. Fencing is expensive but costs can be reduced by using electric fences where appropriate.

Financial commitments to other management priorities will determine the level of shelter establishment for any one year. The most exposed areas should receive priority, but it is acknowledged that while horticultural shelter is essential, farm shelter is merely desirable. In the long term, shelterbelt ages should be staggered so not all belts mature at the same time.

Site Situation: In shelterbelt establishment we are looking for 100% survival, optimum growth for the species and tree stability. To achieve this, four factors have to be taken into account and all four are essential: proper site preparation, selection of good quality stock, correct planting technique, and adequate maintenance. The skill is in achieving a sound root system with a strong tap root and well distributed laterals, like a naturally regenerated tree from seed. Good forestry practice also recognizes these four factors, and much can be learned from experience in this field.

Site Preparation

There are very few sites where shelter can be established successfully without some form of preparation such as weed control, subsoiling, drainage, cultivation or animal control.

Weed Control: To enable sufficient light and moisture to be available to the tree, weeds must be eliminated. When dry conditions occur in late spring and summer, tree deaths are often not directly due to shortage of rain, but more through weed and grass competition for the available moisture. All planting should have some sort of weed control. Development of herbicides over recent years has simplified this task.

The use of the correct chemical for the job at the recommended rates cannot be overemphasized. Desiccant sprays give a quick knock-down effect but do not penetrate to the root system, so some grasses such as dallisgrass and kikuyu will regrow. For these a spray with a translocation ability will be required (i.e. a systemic chemical which will be readily absorbed and transported through the plant system). Residual chemicals can also be used to prevent regrowth but it is of course necessary to ensure that the residue retained in the soil will not affect tree growth. Advice on correct use of chemical weed control is available from manufacturers and advisers and should be sought during the planning stage. Preplanting spraying can be applied as a continuous one meter (3 ft 3 in) strip or as a spot application around each planting position. Minimize spray drift by doing the job on a calm fine day.

Subsoiling: 20-28 inches (to 50-70 cm) should be standard practice on problem soils, with compacted subsoils, hard pans or very stony sites. Even on clay soils subsoiling to a moderate depth has proved worthwhile. Subsoiling gives improved aeration and drainage thus allowing roots to penetrate a larger volume of soil than would have been the case without treatment, thereby increasing vigor and stability. Correct subsoiler design should ensure that a reasonable volume of soil is shattered. If a single tine subsoiler without wings is used, at least two lines 12 inches (30cm) apart should be subsoiled to give a greater shattering effect. (Plant between subsoil trenches.) A single tine subsoiler can cause instability by roots following the line when there is no soil shattering associated with the subsoiler. Subsoiling should be done in the dry season: not when the soil is wet.

Drainage: Poor drainage is always an inhibiting factor in achieving good plant growth, and the same general principles apply for shelterbelts as for other trees (see "Handling and Planting of Trees" chapter). Planting of belts alongside a drain because it saves fencing often seems an easy option. As the root system will not develop on the drain side, instability is almost inevitable especially in soft ground such as peat. This practice is a sure way of building up future problems. If you must plant alongside a drain, always plant on the windward side.

Cultivation by rotary hoeing is often carried out as a means of incorporating extra fertilizers within the soil prior to planting and for weed control. It is often a window dressing and does not greatly help subsequent development if drainage, weeds or soil pan have not been adequately dealt with.

Animal Control: Standard fencing practices used on the farm will suffice for stock but there is no easy way to control feral animals. The most effective way is to eliminate them, otherwise some of the suggestions made in the chapter "Handling and Planting of Trees" may be useful.

Selection of Tree Stocks: This is another crucial area--if tree quality is poor then survival and subsequent tree growth will also be inferior regardless of other techniques used. Remember that in proportion to all other costs (preparation, planting, fertilizing, etc.) tree costs are very small and therefore it is unwise to look for tree stock bargains: there is no such thing in shelter stock.

There are several factors you can check on when ordering stock: first, stem condition which includes height, stem diameter, foliage color, damage by insects and fungi and degree of hardiness; and second, root condition, including fibrous root development and root balance. Mycorrhizal and root damage are observable at the nursery: stock should be checked for these. Third, size of plants: be careful of buying large seedlings as this stock can easily desiccate and may swivel in the wind, causing stem damage. Large seedlings in small containers will have serious root distortion which may lead to strangulation or "hockey stick" root formation with resulting instability.

Sturdy seedlings with a good stem diameter in relation to height do better in terms of survival and subsequent growth than tall seedlings.

The choice of whether to use bare-rooted or container-grown plants will depend on the farmer's personal preference. The merits of each option are discussed in the chapter on "Handling and Planting of Trees." Since fairly large quantities are being handled it must be stressed that good preplanting preparation and a well organized planting program are essential if bare-rooted plants are to be used. Effort is required to ensure good packaging, fast transport and sensible precautions to protect trees from damage or drying out.

Planting

Planting usually commences in late autumn once the soils are moist and goes through to late spring for some varieties. December and January are the best months for bare-rooted stock and for cuttings such as willows and poplars. If the area is subject to hard frosts, then planting of trees should be delayed until the worst frosts are over. Non-suckering bamboo is a species that should be planted as late as April, although because of its shallow rooting it must be irrigated regularly throughout the first summer.

The spacing will determine the speed with which effective early shelter is achieved; it will adversely affect stability, uniformity and height if planting is too close. Cuttings of poplars and willows are generally spaced at 1 ft 7 in to 3 ft 4 in (0.5-1 m) while internal breaks (Australian Pines--*Casuarinas*, also called Horsetail Casuarina or Beefwoods) are often planted at 3 ft 4 in (1 m). The slower growing evergreens such as *Thuja* (Western Redcedar) and *Cupressus* (various cypress species) are best planted at about 6 ft 7.5 in to 8 ft 3 in (2-2.5 m). Fast-growing *Pinus* and *Eucalyptus* for long-term tall shelter should be planted at a minimum of 6 ft 7.5 in (2 m). Multiple-row planting will modify these general spacings, and shelter experience in one region may dictate particular spacing requirements. The actual planting technique varies from site to site, but the greatest success will be achieved when the soil is generally broken up; the seedling is placed upright at a depth no less than the root collar; the roots are evenly spread without cramping and the soil gently firmed about the plant.

Distortion and cramping of the root system may reduce both growth and stability. Deeper planting is recommended where the soils tend to be drought prone, for example sands, volcanic ash and gravelly soils. However, deep planting on often wet, poorly aerated deep clay soils could be disastrous. A spade or mattock is normally used to prepare each hole for planting; however a post-hole borer may also be used providing the sides are well spaded out to allow future root penetration.

Should container-grown plants exhibit any root distortion, simply cut off any coils and make four vertical slits to enable roots to be freed. Trim off any damaged roots as these can allow pathogens to enter and cause root rot.

Cuttings are usually driven into the ground or alternatively a crowbar can be used to make a hole. A black polythene mulch can be employed to create a warmer soil temperature, to conserve moisture and to prevent weed growth around the cutting. An angled cut at the base of the cutting will make penetration through the plastic and into the soil much easier. Shoot growth from the cutting depends on moisture and nutrient reserves held within the wood until roots are sufficiently well developed to sustain shoot growth. Therefore standing cuttings in water for 7-10 days before planting can contribute to survival. The more of the cutting inserted in the ground the better the early root development and reduction in dehydration. Generally cuttings should be planted with about two-thirds of their length firmly in the soil.

Fertilizer can be incorporated at time of planting, applied either in the last cultivation prior to plastic mulching (if used) or as a slow-release fertilizer placed in the planting hole and thoroughly mixed into the soil before planting. Most plants will benefit from a well-balanced fertilizer such as blood and bone or crop mix 6:6:5. However, soil tests or advice from agricultural advisers will be able to confirm a suitable fertilizer program for a particular locality. Fertilizers applied too close to the stem or in contact with the roots will cause root burn and often death to the seedling. Remember that most shelterbelts are planted on land previously in production and manured in the past. It is not to be assumed that fertilizer is required.

Maintenance

Factors adversely affecting growth after establishment are lack of moisture, infertility, disease and animal damage.

Moisture competition is a major reason why many shelter lines never become effective. Proper weed control after planting, undertaken by hand, by mulching or with herbicides may be necessary for a number of years depending on the growth rates of the species used.

Mulches of untreated sawdust, bark, or both, about 4-6 inches (10-15 cm) thick along the shelter line after killing all perennial weeds, can be a very cheap form of weed control. A scattering of blood and bone applied before mulching replaces nitrogen used in decomposition. Care should be taken not to heap mulch about the seedling stem as abrasion damage and stem rot may occur.

Weeds can still be controlled by herbicides even after planting, but these are dangerous to young trees if applied incorrectly. Avoid drift onto trees by using low-pressure applicators with a shield to the spray boom, or cover plants at time of spraying. (See also earlier recommendations on weed control.)

Where moisture is limiting to good growth, proper weed control should ensure survival but the addition of irrigation will increase growth. Low-pressure systems such as trickle irrigation are now commonly used throughout the horticultural industry. The effect of irrigation is greatest in the initial years of establishment when the developing seedling requires good moisture availability. Different species have varying sensitivity to moisture stress; for example, *Eucalyptus* will tolerate high moisture stress whereas willows and poplars need abundant rates of available moisture to maintain good growth rates. Trickle irrigation requires clean water together with good design to ensure correct pipe sizes, positions and flow rates, and these factors should be considered at the early planning stage.

Depending on the natural soil fertility and how much basal dressing has already been applied, side dressing may not be required. There is some benefit in notching the fertilizer into the soil to reduce nutrient losses and ensuring application is about 6 inches (15 cm) away from the seedling to prevent any burning effect. Don't overdo it--get good local advice as various soils and tree species have markedly different requirements.

Control of lateral spread by regular side trimming, especially in poplars, willows and *Casuarinas* will keep trees narrow, porous, wind-firm and prevent gaps developing underneath. Evergreen varieties are best trimmed in late summer or early spring at times of vigorous growth. Trimming little and often will maintain internal shelter and reduce the risk of die-back. In horticulture blocks deep root pruning is now being found necessary to counter lateral expansion of the root system into the productive areas.

Disease

Nearly all shelter species can be affected by various pests and diseases, although if healthy seedlings and good establishment techniques are used then any disease problems will be minimal. The types of diseases that are relatively common among shelter trees can be corrected without too much trouble providing precautions are taken before serious loss occurs.

• Black beetle and grass grub are major pests on farmland, affecting roots and causing severe losses. Post-planting treatment with organophosphates will control them.

• White crown canker will affect most shelter trees although some species are more resistant to canker than others. It will kill clusters of trees, spreading to adjacent trees to produce serious gaps. Plant resistant species.

• Root diseases such as *Phytophthora* and *Pythium* cause death by killing fibrous roots. These can be a problem where the site is poorly drained and where plants have been physically damaged at planting time. Proper site preparation and careful planting will restrict this problem.

• Cypress canker, result of a fungus attack, causes severe dieback (e.g. Lawson's Cypress and Leyland Cypress). Avoid planting susceptible species in areas where this disease is endemic.

• Needle cast disease in pines is less common in shelter planting than in a forest situation, however spraying with copper-based fungicides to control the disease in the first 3-6 years may be required.

• Leaf roller damage can severely limit growth of some *Eucalyptus* species by chewing out branch and leader tips. Spraying with insecticides during spring and autumn may be necessary for control.

Other disorders such as leaf spotting fungi (*Cryptomeria*), silver leaf disease (poplars, willows and *Eucalyptus*) and mite damage (*Cryptomeria*) can all be easily controlled if noticed early during routine health inspections. (Note: *Cryptomeria* or Japanese Cedar is native to Japan and some parts of China. It is used in New Zealand for windbreaks and shelterbelts. This evergreen can grow in cold conditions and thrives in districts where winter temperatures reach -11°C. It does best in good, moist soils and in reasonably sheltered situations. Propagation is from seed or from cuttings.)

Cold

If you lose enough heat from your body core, you die. So do animals. Strong winds accompanied by low temperatures cause rapid cooling of exposed surfaces of the body in both people and livestock. A strong wind combined with a temperature slightly below freezing can have the same effect as a temperature which is nearly 20°C (70°F) lower.

Anyone who is outdoors during low temperatures and strong winds will find he or she becomes exhausted easily and is more subject to frostbite or even death. Stockmen and stockwomen likewise should consider the effect of the wind chill factor on unprotected livestock during cold strong winds.

Table showing effect of wind on temperature

° C	calm	15 mph 24 km/h	30 mph 48 km/h	40 mph 64km/h
-1.1°C	-1.1°C	-11.7°C	-18.9°C	-20°C
-6.7	-6.7	-21.1	-27.8	-30
-12.2	-12.2	-27.8	-36.1	-37.8
-17.8	-17.8	-36.1	-45	-47.7
-23.3	-23.3	-42.8	-52.7	-56.1
-28.9	-28.9	-51.1	-61.1	-66.1
-34.4	-34.4	-56.7	-70.0	-73.8
-40	-40	-62.2	-78.3	-82.2

Wind speeds greater than 40 mph (64 km/h)
have little additional chilling effect.

Snow Shelter

One major limiting factor in farm production is the lack of shelter during snow storms.

Shelter in these situations has to be designed to cope with drifting snow. A fall of only 4 inches (10 cm) accompanied by strong winds can cause major drifts. Even when the storm has passed, the wind can still cause drifting. A conventional one or two row shelterbelt has the effect of collecting the snow in the sheltered area. These belts are then of no value--when needed most they become deathtraps for livestock.

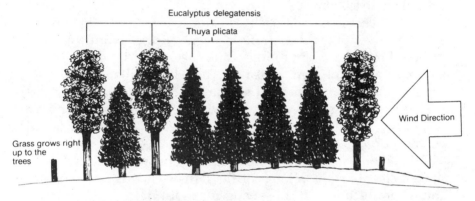

In this multi-row shelterbelt snow cannot drift on to the leeward side. The inside trees form the woodlot and could be Douglas Fir, *Pinus nigra* or *Pinus radiata*.

The gulley traps drifting snow,
and good shelter is provided on the leeward side of the trees.

There are two ways that the snow can be stopped before reaching the sheltered area:

1. By having a multi-row belt, wide enough to trap all the snow in the actual belt.

2. By having a gully fenced into the belt on the windward side. The snow drifts into the gully and the trees downwind provide the shelter for the stock, hay feeding area etc.

The second method is preferred because as well as taking what could be a dangerous gully out of the paddock, the whole shelterbelt area can be grazed over the summer months once the trees have reached a suitable height.

While these shelterbelts do not follow the design of the permeable windbreaks that are in vogue further North [in New Zealand], they are appropriate and necessary in these colder Southern areas [of New Zealand]. The windchill factor increases dramatically once windspeed gets above 3 mph (5 km/hour). As well as controlling the snow, these wide belts also provide an area where wind spread is near zero and where newborn lambs and newly shorn sheep can survive the roughest weather.

When winter storms are over and lambing is finished these shelterbelts are still working for the farmer--increasing grass and animal production and conserving soil moisture.

Multiple Use of Shelter

Shelterbelts can provide useful timber and fencing material for on-farm use as well as providing valuable stock/crop shelter. There has been an increasing awareness of multiple land use over recent years and timber production is just one extra reward with minimal additional input. Timber from shelterbelts is by no means a new concept.

By proper selection of species and correctly applied management techniques a shelterbelt can be designed for timber production. Because timber-producing species are suitable for shelter planting, long-term management (30-40 years) will produce a valuable wood resource. Just how valuable depends on the level of management, that is selective pruning and thinning. In managing a shelterbelt we need to maintain porosity and prevent any serious gaps developing. A pruning technique must ensure the maintenance of the shelter design. The simplest plan is to establish multiple rows, using two different species. Slow-growing trees planted on the side of the prevailing wind become ultimately tall primary shelter, replacing the faster-growing trees when these are harvested.

Examples of two-row general purpose, permeable shelterbelts.
Species choice and spacing depend on region and local site characteristics.
[Note, * ornamental, not normally grown in North America.]

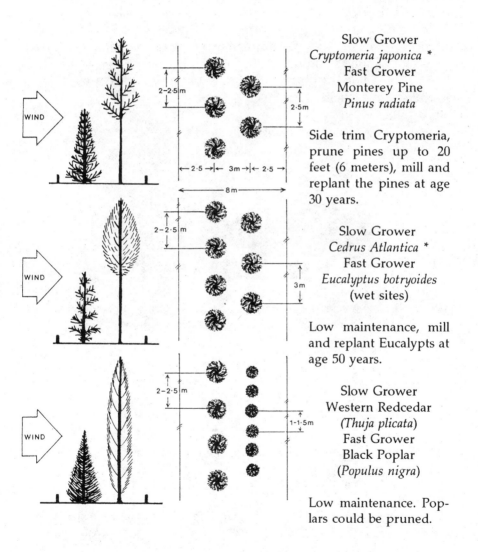

Slow Grower
Cryptomeria japonica *
Fast Grower
Monterey Pine
Pinus radiata

Side trim Cryptomeria, prune pines up to 20 feet (6 meters), mill and replant the pines at age 30 years.

Slow Grower
Cedrus Atlantica *
Fast Grower
Eucalyptus botryoides
(wet sites)

Low maintenance, mill and replant Eucalypts at age 50 years.

Slow Grower
Western Redcedar
(*Thuja plicata*)
Fast Grower
Black Poplar
(*Populus nigra*)

Low maintenance. Poplars could be pruned.

Allowing for site and soil limitations, the aim should be to produce timber of a quality acceptable to the market. The higher the quality, the better return to be made at harvesting time. However, quality timber is generally associated with defect-free (clear-wood) timber which is usually a result of wood grown outside a core of pruned branch stubs. But the principles of pruning (removing all branches up the stem of the tree to a determined height) is in opposition to the principles of good shelter, i.e. maintaining a gap-free belt. Therefore if pruning is to be considered, the design and management must compensate for the effect of such pruning.

The following diagram suggests methods for the production of timber from shelterbelts.

Management of shelterbelts for timber

(a) Plant timber species, no management. This system will provide timber of lower quality than the following options.

(b) Prune every second tree. Every second tree will produce a proportion of defect-free timber, while branches from neighboring trees will overlap to provide even porosity.

View from above

(c) Fan prune all trees. (Fan pruning is the pruning of branches growing at right angles to the line of the shelterbelt.) This system is akin to trimming but branches are removed flush with the stem. Shading over the fence is reduced while good porosity is maintained. Some increase in timber quality is also gained.

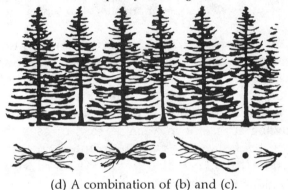

(d) A combination of (b) and (c).

(e) Prune all trees. All trees producing clearwood butt logs but the design must allow for the holes to be filled by another unpruned row and/or another species. An alternative (less intensive management) is using a recognized self pruning species such as eucalypts (although these still need some pruning of persistent branches in a shelterbelt situation) with the gaps filled in by another species.

(f) Prune every second set of branches up to the stem to create long clear lengths of timber between whorls. A method of increasing porosity as well as some improvement to timber yield.

When two species are considered for planting, by the careful selection of a fast- and slow-growing species, timber production is made easier. The fast-growing species can be pruned for clearwood production while the second species should have grown enough to fill the gaps, either by planting alternately with the fast-growing species if in a single row, or as a second row. (Secondary species should always be planted on the windward side.) The more rows of timber-producing species planted, the closer the management comes to that of a woodlot. Also, the more rows planted, the denser the belt becomes. This requires more management to maintain a porous shelterbelt and thus effective shelter. Firewood production is another management alternative. To maintain optimum structure multiple rows of say Monterey Pines (*Pinus radiata*), or cedar (*Cedrus* species), cypress (*Cupressus* species), or juniper (*Juniperus* species) will produce thinnings, which can be used as a fuel wood.

Soil Erosion

The top few centimeters of soil are usually richest in nutrients and organisms, which make the nutrients available to plants, as well as being the most physically suitable for seed germination. Hence any removal of this soil by wind depletes the cropping capability of the site.

Alarming examples of soil erosion emphasize how necessary it is to plant trees not only to shelter man, beast and crop, but also to protect the very substance of a country's productive capacity.

A Few Thoughtful Tree Tips

● On a very exposed farm, Pampas Grass (*Cortaderia selloana*) protected by electric fences makes effective low shelter.

● Some shelterbelts can be more effective when two species are planted together.

● To create a two-row shelterbelt, plant slow-growing Arizona Cypress (*Cupressus arizonica*) on the windward side of your farm and pruned Monterey Pine (*Pinus radiata*) on the leeward side.

● Poplars underplanted with pampas make a most effective windbreak.

● To enhance the beauty of a shelterbelt, plant a shelter of evergreen trees running North and South down a ridge. On the eastern side of this shelterbelt, plant various oaks whose brilliantly colored leaves show up in autumn against the evergreens.

● Poor fencing can cause drafty and uneven shelter.

● Willows can be closely planted as shelter for horticulture. With irrigation they grow extremely fast.

● Willows can be used to start controlling serious erosion of volcanic soils.

4: Shade

It was Noel Coward who drew attention to the peculiar behavior of colonials when he sang of mad dogs and Englishmen going out in the midday sun. Farmers everywhere still do it today, and subject their farm animals to the same conditions. Few farms have adequate shade for the comfort of their stock. Their distress on really hot days is plain to see. You will have observed the pathetic attempts of sheep seeking relief from the hot sun in the shade of a solitary power pole, or settling into the minute cover given by an unwanted and unloved nodding thistle.

If livestock are happier and more contented when provided with shade, this is surely justification for providing it. People use it around their homes and occasionally a tree or two is grown to provide more comfortable conditions in the stockyards--not usually for the benefit of the stock, but rather for the worker. Contented stock make for contented stockmen, and stock suffering from stress--whatever form it might take--tend to transmit that stress to the stockman.

Humane considerations aside, overseas research suggests that there can be an economic gain from shade. Research by Shingoro Moda in Taiwan discovered the following:

"All farm animals, sheep, cattle and pigs, are homeotherms. They attempt to maintain their body temperatures within the range most suitable for their optimum biological activity. Under hot conditions an animal's ability to regulate its body temperature depends on an effective evaporative heat loss mechanism. In European cattle no demands are made on the temperature-regulating mechanisms between 32°F/0°C and 60°/15°C. After this there is a rapid increase in respiration and vaporization rates. At about 84°F/27°C these mechanisms begin to fail as shown by the abrupt rise in rectal temperature, decline in food production, milk production and body weight. Heat stress in cattle is reflected in lowered food consumption, and as a result, productivity is affected in cows. Adverse changes occur in yield and composition of milk. The critical temperature for milk yield decline appears to be between 72°F/21°C and 84°F/27°C for Holsteins and Jerseys.

"The deleterious effect of hot weather on farm animals necessitates sheltering them from heat, including sun radiation. This is best done by trees because their leaves are cooled by vaporization from their surfaces.

Contented stock make stockmen contented.

"With air temperature ranging from 60-94°F/15-32°C Jerseys and Holsteins sought shade at about 84°F/27°C. On days when shade temperature was 88°F/29°C they spent only 11% of their time grazing. At night when temperature was 84°F/27°C, 37% of their time was spent grazing."

University of Florida research discovered: "The difference of 0.14 pound daily weight gain in favor of steers having access to shade was 'significant' (mainly steers of British breeding). Shade had no effect on carcass grade or dressing percentage and there were no significant differences in feed required for gain."

A study conducted on the Southern Plains Experimental Range in Woodward, Oklahoma, found: "Shade increased summer-long gain of yearling Hereford steers on rangeland by a profitable 19 lb (8.6 kg)/head in a 4 year study. High summer humidity depressed steer gains much more than did high summer temperature. The combined effects of humidity above 45% and temperature above 85°F/27°C were especially harmful. Each 'hot muggy day' reduced summer-long steer gains by 1 lb (.45 kg). Cattle eagerly sought shade during hot summer days. By manipulating shade, cattle were drawn to underutilized areas of pasture to reduce damaging spot grazing. Shade was nearly as effective as water location and supplemental feeding as a tool to promote uniform grazing within a pasture. South facing, open sheds used as winter shelters did not increase steer gains, nor would the steers use them even during storms."

Above 15°C/60°F there is a rapid increase
in respiration and vaporization rates.

Researcher J. Hancock noted the following: "At temperatures above 70°F/21.1°C milk yield decreases slowly at first, but after 80°F/26.7°C there is a sudden drop."

"On the basis of the reviews written over the last 20 years the conclusion that high environmental temperature reduces productive and reproductive efficiency of livestock seems well justified," wrote J.W. Fuquay in the **Journal of Animal Science**.

The greatest economic benefits provided by shade appear to be to the dairy farmer because milk yield and quality start to deteriorate at 72°F/21°C, but as temperature climbs the beef grazier also benefits.

Of concern to many who have studied the situation is the stress to which deer are being subjected with their removal to unsheltered and unshaded environments. They have similar regulatory mechanisms to other ruminant domesticated animals but are less equipped to handle the farm situation because they have not had generations of conditioning to it. They are accustomed to living on forest fringes where they can duck for cover or seek shade and shelter at their convenience. Farmers pluck them from this natural environment and force them to live in small open paddocks where they spend their lives in an almost perpetual state of tension, running for non-existent cover at the slightest alarm and sheltered by nothing more than a netting fence.

This handling of deer reflects a degree of insensitivity almost equal to factory farming of pigs or hens. It might be difficult to change the latter situations, but we can do much to alleviate deer stress by planting trees. Fenced-off corners not only allow the tree to be protected but the longer grass which will grow around it will provide cover for newborn fawns, provided the bottom wire or board is fixed high enough off the ground. The huge financial investments being made in deer surely justify a greater consideration for their welfare.

There are a number of diseases in which the skin of affected animals becomes unduly sensitive to sunlight. The most common of these is facial eczema which affects sheep and cattle. The extreme discomfort suffered by affected animals which are forced to stay in the sun is a most distressing sight. There is no cure for facial eczema but the unhappy lot of the sick animal will be relieved if it has access to shade and this may well help in its eventual recovery through its own natural processes.

The relevance of what has been written can best be illustrated by reference to the meteorological records. However it should be borne in mind that it is not temperature alone that triggers off adverse effects. A trial in Midwestern USA indicated that there are four environmental factors that can stress feedlot cattle if these factors are at a high level: average minimum air temperature; average maximum air temperature; average radiant heat load; number of hours above 89°F/29.5°C.

It is fairly clear that once air temperatures go above 72°F/21°C there are adverse effects on most farm animals. If these temperatures are coupled with other undesirable environment factors then the effect is compounded. It is a commonly held belief that temperature as measured in the sun is higher than that in the shade. There is in fact no difference. It is the difference in the radiation absorbed by the animal in the two different situations which determines the degree of stress.

When trees are used to provide shade there is no reason why the same trees cannot also provide timber and beauty too. Plantings of dense evergreens are normally unsuitable as they result in less winter sun and loss of too much pasture; they also encourage stock camping. Typical of appropriate tree types are the Black Poplar hybrids, which are quite happy without the company of others. Pruned up to 20 ft (6m) they can eventually provide saw logs and will during the intervening years give excellent shade. Grass grows right up to their base, and during the winter, sunlight will be allowed onto the pasture. The high pruning of any shade tree is important, for it results in the area of shade moving around the paddock as the day goes by. Thus there is no over-use of any one area by the animals and the grass sward remains undamaged.

(**The Encyclopedia of Organic Gardening**, Rodale Books Inc., describes accumulator plants as those which have an ability to collect trace elements from the soil with storage in their tissues of several hundred times the amount contained in an equal weight of soil. It lists poplar and hickory leaves and peach tree clippings as accumulators of zinc. Used as shade trees it might be possible that they could contribute enough zinc to reduce the incidence of facial eczema.)

Another Thoughtful Tree Tip

• When pruning, pruned branches should be cut off flush with the trunk of a tree. This aids occlusion. Branches that are not closely pruned will never heal, possibly resulting in disease.

North American Notes

• Dot single trees randomly in a pasture so that animals will have more than one location to seek shade, or plant along fencelines.

• Plant trees on slopes to aid water runoff after rains. This also lowers the opportunity for parasites to breed in muddy environments. In dry weather slopes become dust bowls where worm eggs and lice can spread.

• Erect a fence protector several feet from the tree trunk to protect roots from animal damage.

• If feasible, plant shade-tolerant grasses such as bahaia beneath trees.

• To optimize grass growth plant deciduous trees in East-West rows for maximum sunlight exposure and evergreens in North-South rows.

5: Trees for Birds, Bees and Browse

For the Birds

It seems important to include in this book a few suggestions as to how the rural landowner can help preserve the bird
population. We tend to take birds for granted. It is sometimes
necessary to be in a place entirely devoid of birdlife before it is
brought home just how much we accept as part of our normal life
the birdsong of night and morning.

Directly or indirectly, trees and shrubs provide many of the
basic requirements--food, shelter, escape, cover, and suitable
nesting places.

Generally it will be found that deciduous trees tend to
attract and hold birds more than evergreens, although planting of
any tree that can provide a food source for birds should be worthwhile. Look to berried trees and shrubs if you want to encourage
the birds to stay around your farm.

Any tree or shrub will have some value to some bird, but
to get the best possible results from planting you have to be
selective. A year-round supply of food is often the most serious
limiting factor. If you provide this, particularly for fruit and nectar
feeders, the same trees in sufficient variety will also provide most
other requirements, including food for insect- and seed-eaters.
Selection must of course be influenced by local climate and
conditions.

Apart from trees, you can also establish feeding stations
handy to the house. These can be supplied with mutton fat, lard,
nectar or sugar liquid and household scraps which will provide
additional food for birds, particularly during winter when natural
food resources are low. [One handy tip for disposing of rendered
kitchen fat is to let it form a jell in the refrigerator and then roll
pine cones in it for the birds.]

Once again it is pertinent to point out that so many trees can serve a dual purpose. Should you decide to plant a tree specifically for birds it will be unlikely that you cannot find one which will serve another purpose on the farm, be it long-term timber, shelter or beauty.

Establishing trees on effluent pond surrounds will attract birds to the site and make an improvement in the appearance of the area.

Here are a few species that attract birds:
Firethorn (*Pyracantha coccinea*)
Hawthorns (*Crataegus*)
Silky-oak (*Grevillea robusta*)
Prunus species, which include crabapple, cherry, plum, among many fruit species.

And the Bees

This section is included because many farmers have a special interest in bees. Since they are essential to the reproduction of plant species it is important for them to have a plentiful supply of food. A good percentage of our diet comes directly from plants requiring insect pollination or indirectly from animals which are fed largely on insect-pollinated crops. Honey bees are by far the most important and numerous of these pollinators.

Honey bees need protein, which they obtain from pollen, and carbohydrates, which they obtain from nectar. The critical period in the beekeeping cycle is the spring when the hive is expanding but the main flow of nectar is not usually available.

A healthy honey bee colony will rear in one year between 100,000 and 200,000 bees. This requires 30-50 kg (66-110 lbs) of pollen, and to collect this amount each hive will have to bring in 2-4 million bee loads of pollen. It has also been calculated that it requires 144,000-160,000 bee trips to gather and produce one kilogram (2.205 lbs) of honey. The bee requires a large amount of energy to carry out this self-imposed task, and since the energy is provided by the carbohydrates the provision of nectar is vital.

In some areas land development has produced a sterile environment which will no longer support enough bee colonies to carry out all the pollination that is required. Elsewhere too, removal of noxious weeds has aggravated the scarcity of food sources. Willows along stream banks have been an excellent source of early pollen and nectar but in the interests of flood control these are being cut down. The more the natural food supplies disappear the greater the dependence there is on artificial feeding and the higher the cost of maintaining a hive, provided it even stays in the area.

The planting of nectar- and pollen-bearing trees is therefore important and there is every possibility that such a program can be compatible with and complementary to other planting objectives. Many trees used for beauty, timber, erosion control and shelter can provide bee fodder at a time when it is most required, i.e. when pasture flowers, which provide most bee requirements, are not yet in bloom, or when drought has taken its toll.

In addition to offering a food source, shelter creates a better environment for bee aeronautics, and if there are no headwinds to battle against (especially tiresome with a load on) the bee may well increase the number of daily trips. The necessity of providing bees for pollination of kiwifruit has dramatically illustrated the important role of this most energetic and productive insect and how essential it is to pastoral and horticultural economies.

Bee Food Sources

Key: Np Used by bees more as a nectar than pollen source
Pn Used by bees more as a pollen than nectar source
P Pollen source only
NP Equally valuable for nectar and pollen

Spring/Early Summer
Sycamore Maple (*Acer pseudo-platanus*) Np
Common Privet (*Ligustrum vulgare*) Np
Common Apple (*Malus domestica*) Np
Pear (*Pyrus* species) P
Black Locust (*Robinia pseudo-acacia*) NP

Summer
Honey Locust (*Gleditsia triacanthos*) Pn
Peru Pepper Tree (*Schinus molle*) Np
Linden (*Tilia* species) Np

Winter/Early Spring
Peach (*Prunus persica*) Pn
Apricot, Cherry, Plum (*Prunus* species) Pn

Weeping Willow (*Salix babylonica*) NP
Goat Willow (*Salix caprea*) Pn
Crack Willow (*Salix fragilis*) NP

[A few additional North American trees that can provide food sources for bees include arrowwoods (*Viburnum* species), basswoods (*Tilia* species), mesquites (*Prosopis* species), Persimmon (*Diospyros virginiana*), Sourwood (*Oxydendrum arboreum*), the Tulip Poplar or Tulip-tree (*Liriodendron tulipifera*), and Tupelo (*Nyssa aquatica*).]

North American Notes:
Browse for Domestic Stock

Browse (woody plants) makes up a large and very valuable forage component in North America especially in the more arid regions. Sheep and goat production has tended to concentrate in these arid regions as the plentiful browse eliminated the need for winter feeding. Unlike grasses, the food values of browse plants remain high for most of the year. This is particularly true of the proteins and sugars.

Abundant, large-leafed browse can be utilized to a surprising extent by beef cattle, particularly if they have a sizable percentage of Brahman breeding. However, browse is better utilized by small-mouthed, selective grazing sheep and goats than cattle. Cattle with their large mouths will frequently wind up with as much limb as leaf.

The fine-wooled sheep breeds, such as the Merino, are better browsers than the coarse-wooled breeds. Sheep primarily utilize browse during the fall and winter when their preferred diet of fine grasses and weeds are in short supply. Goats can utilize browse year-round but need green and succulent weeds and grasses after kidding to keep milk production adequate.

Goats prefer to graze on plants higher than their heads. This is their way of naturally preventing parasitism. Goats are extremely susceptible to internal parasitism in humid environments and should only be used in areas where there is access to plenty of parasite-free browse. Goats make excellent companion grazers to beef stocker cattle in humid environments but should not be combined with sheep in humid environments as they are highly susceptible to sheep internal parasites.

In arid environments, a planned species rotation, or a mixture of sheep, cattle and goats is better than any one species alone. Care must be taken in these regions not to overuse the type of forage most desirable for the animals produced. An overgrazed sheep range can change from one producing numerous weeds and fine grasses to one producing only coarse grasses and brush. In other words, a range better suited to cattle and goats. Similarly, the browse plants so essential in goat operations can be quickly eliminated by too heavy grazing and create a range better suited for sheep and goats.

In arid regions, sheep and/or goats should always be the centerpiece, or dominant activity, rather than beef cattle. Their superior browsing ability makes a much better use of the range resources than cattle. Conversely, sheep and/or goats should never be the centerpiece in humid regions due to their high susceptibility to internal parasites. Cattle which are more resistant to their own parasites and immune to those of sheep and goats should be the centerpiece in humid climates.

Sheep and pecans make ideal companions. The husk of the pecan is an excellent sheep feed and sheep readily eat it. The natural dehusking and close-grazing pattern of sheep facilitate the pecan nut harvest. The light weight of the sheep does not contribute to soil compaction and the understory pasture and the pecan trees both benefit from the same fertilization regimen.

In the Pacific Northwest where herbicide use is restricted on U.S. Forest Service land, sheep graze replanted clear-cut forest areas and keep down the grass. This integration saves not only money but the environment.

Merino wethers (castrated males) have been used in pine plantations in the Eastern USA. Unlike reproducing females that need quality pasture at various stages of their lives, the nutritional requirements of wethers vary little, making them especially suitable for use in pine plantations. Integrating sheep into pine plantations would work well in the hilly areas of southeastern Ohio where there is abandoned farmland and some mined areas.

Finally, shearing ewes prior to lambing will force them into sheltered areas where their lambs will have a much better chance of survival.

North American Notes:
Browse for Deer and Wildlife

● Beef cattle periodically turned into the woods can freshen up wildlife browse, greatly improving deer nutrition and antler growth.

● Deer are attracted to the seeds, buds and twigs of trees that belong in the aspen, cedar, cottonwood, dogwood, holly, maple, mesquite, and poplar families, among other species.

● Willows, which deer and wildlife use for browse, can make an excellent drought reserve for livestock. They should be strip-grazed with a moveable electric fence. After grazing they should be cut off at a six-inch height (15 cm) and allowed to regrow before grazing again.

6: Mast and Other Matters

North American Notes:

In Defense of Pastured Pigs

I admit to being an enthusiast of the pastured pig. Yes, unmanaged pigs can root up tree seedlings, dig holes in the pasture and ransack your neighbor's garden. However, in this era of high-powered electric fences we can now put a pig where we want him and be assured he will stay there. Pigs hate electric fences. In fact, a major management problem is to get the pig to cross a place where an electric fence used to be.

While pastured pigs can be a profitable, centerpiece enterprise, this requires the growing of grain crops for hogging off or large purchases of grain and protein supplement. I prefer my pastured pig to be a total scavenger. I want him to live on table scraps, acorns, clover, wild pecans, chestnuts, locust pods, snakes, rotting apples and pears, wild blackberries, pasture grubs, persimmons and mulberries. This is why pigs work well with fodder trees that are planted for shade or shelter.

I want there to be enough food resources available on top of the ground so that he doesn't have to root. Maybe I have only two or three pigs. Maybe only one. Maybe I give him a coffee can of corn once a week to remind him he is still a domestic pig and has not been returned to the wild. Maybe I miss a week feeding him every now and then. I don't want this to be a big deal.

As anyone who has ever watched a pig on pasture, pigs love to eat cow manure! And, it's good for them! The University of Missouri found cow manure to be the ideal vitamin and mineral package for a pig. Why more people can't see the beneficial parasite-cleansing effect a few pastured pigs could produce is beyond me. Also, if lightning should accidentally bop a cow, your paddock pigs will gladly dispose of her carcass for you before the smell can attract the coyotes.

I want to buy my pastured pig in the early spring at around 200 lbs and send him on his way to whole-hog sausage heaven in the late fall. At 200 pounds he can make his way on pasture without any protein supplement. Yeah, I know a 200 pound pig is a hog, but it is not alliterative with pasture.

Did you know in the 1920s there was a huge mulberry-hog-grazing industry in the Carolinas? One mulberry tree will feed one hog for three months! But what's a mulberry's berry worth without a pig? The value of the annual crop of nuts and mast our trees produce are totally lost to us without pigs and in the case of acorns can actually endanger our cattle.

Pigs are more fun to watch than cable TV. There is no animal more entertaining than a pastured pig doing his thing. Anyone who has ever seen the joy of a pig on pasture could never stand to see another one raised in confinement. Louis Bromfield said that to be financially successful at raising pigs, one had to learn to think like a pig. He warned that much of the "expert" advice given on raising pigs is given by people who could never possibly imagine themselves as a pig.

You will probably never hear an "expert" recommend a pastured pig to you. You don't spend any money on them so there's no profit in them for any off-farm corporation. They are very unscientific. They aren't in the least fashionable. They even smack of third-worldism. But add up all the benefits and remember, if your neighbors don't think what you're doing is crazy, you'll never make any money farming. Go for it!

North American Notes:
A Word of Warning about Acorns

While acorns produce ample forage for hogs, they can be deadly to cattle. Young cattle that weigh less than 450 pounds are the most susceptible since their digestive system is not equipped to detoxify the tannins acorns contain, but even mature cattle can be poisoned.

All edible parts of the oak tree--acorns, buds, leaves and limbs--contain this toxic tannin.

If cattle are removed from the source and treated soon enough they may recover within two months. Untreated cattle usually die within a week or two of symptoms becoming obvious.

Symptoms of oak poisoning include:

- Lower than normal temperature.
- Irregular heart beat.
- Digestive tract and kidney malfunctions.
- Edema or dropsy under the jaw and belly.
- Little or no voiding of urine or manure.
- Bloodshot eyes as uremic poisoning develops.
- Breath that smells of ammonia.

Treatment by a veterinarian may include intravenous fluid therapy to promote kidney function and correct electrolyte abnormalities; diuretics administered every 12 hours to help cattle void better while antibiotics help nurse sick calves back to health. Experiments have also been done by adding calcium hydroxide (hydrated lime) to feed. (Cattle will eat feed containing 10% or less of calcium hydroxide.)

Farmers who have trouble keeping cattle out of oak woods can try feeding two pounds per head per day of a cubed or pelleted supplement that contains 10% hydrated lime.

North American Notes:
In Praise of the Honey Locust

If ever there was a wonder tree for farms with livestock, the Honey Locust (*Gleditsia triacanthos*) is it. Not only will it provide forage, shelter, shade, and stout, long-lasting fence posts, but it will grow in all but the most arid areas of the USA. Honey Locusts are good, durable, fast-growing, forage-producing shelterbelts in the prairie states. Side benefits are habitats for birds within its boughs, autumn color, and thorny branches that cattle utilize as a favored back scratch.

After the first frost, the Honey Locust drops its beans, which make both fine wintergrazing for pigs and cattle and tasty food for people as well. One mature Honey Locust will produce up to 10 bushels of high quality forage beans suitable for dairy cows, beef fattening stock, or pigs.

Research at Auburn University in 1945 showed that Honey Locust beans were pound for pound as good as oats for dairy cattle and that at a stocking rate of 35 trees to the acre Honey Locust could produce a yield equivalent of 275 bushels of oats to the acre while growing two and a half tons of Sericea lespedeza hay to the acre between the trees as well! The only drawback is that they can form a dense thicket. However, over a number of years they will thin themselves sufficiently for a grass sward to thrive underneath.

There are grafted varieties of Honey Locust that produce an abundance of large fleshy pods that contain up to 29% sugar, which are highly palatable to livestock. The pod yield of an appropriately spaced planting can be equivalent to an equal area planted to oats, and this does not include the understory forage production. Grafted stock has the additional advantage of being largely free of thorns.

North American Notes:
More Forage from Trees

Black Walnut (*Juglans nigra*), Black Locust (*Robinia pseudoacacia*), and Honey Locust are the most compatible hardwoods for integration with grazing. They all leaf out relatively late in the spring. They lose leaves relatively early in the fall, and have fairly open canopies that allow sufficient light through during the summer to maintain some growth by a forage understory. They also have compound leaves that quickly settle through a forage canopy in the autumn and decay, thereby eliminating any potential for leaves smothering the understory. The leaves are unpalatable to cattle, but can be grazed when young.

Black Walnut tree roots secrete a compound called jugolene, which is toxic to many plants but not to the most popular cool-season pasture species. Research in Ohio found that forage production was higher and of better quality under Black Walnuts due to the lack of weed competition. This lack of weeds was attributed to the effect of jugolene.

Research in southern Missouri at one site showed an increase in forage yield and forage quality in a 35-year-old Black Walnut stand compared to a similar site without trees. The reason for this is not certain, but one could speculate that during the hot, dry Missouri summer, the deep rooted trees did not compete heavily with the forage understory for near-surface soil water, while providing shade to lessen forage water utilization. The trees undoubtedly provided a cooler, more desirable environment for cool-season forages during the summer, yet had no substantial impact on spring forage production.

Black Locust is a nitrogen-fixing legume that thrives on poor quality, acidic soils. It is widely planted on strip mine soils. It can improve pasture yields by contributing nitrogen and cycling other soil nutrients from the deeper soil profile. Its wood is very dense and rot resistant and is highly prized for fence post material.

Trees with deep tap roots bring up trace elements that may be missing in the pasture. Cattle or sheep that select for woody plant parts rather than the vegetative part of the plant are probably mineral deficient. Have your forage (not your soil) analyzed and see what is missing so that you can add it to your pasture fertilization program.

Some Southwestern readers may be taken aback to learn that the mesquite bean will readily fatten cows, horses, goats, pigs, and will do this in August when range quality is in decline. The leguminous mesquite tree or Honey Mesquite (*Prosopis glandulosus*) also contributes nitrogen to the surrounding grasses and produces long-lasting fence posts for the pasture fence. By the way, the name mesquite is believed to be of Aztec Indian origin. Not surprisingly, Native Americans used the ground up seeds for breadmaking and fermented drinks.

7: Handling and Planting of Trees

Nothing kills enthusiasm quicker than a succession of planting failures, so it is important to follow correct procedures to assure success. There are many unavoidable factors affecting survival without adding failures caused by shoddy or careless planting. You are making an investment in labor and money so it is worth taking a little extra care right at the beginning.

Protectors

The rural landowner has special problems to cope with. Of all of them the most important is protection from animals, be they domestic such as cattle, sheep, deer, goats and horses (the worst enemies) or feral animals such as opossums, hares/rabbits and goats. The first piece of advice is to get your protector up first and plant your tree later. It is too easy to get carried away when in a nursery and buy more than you have planned for. You must resist the temptation to plant out trees intending to put up protectors later or before you move your stock in.

Stock protectors come in a great variety of styles, but there is one feature they all have in common--they are unattractive and do nothing to enhance the beauty of a tree. Some very expensive and imposing wooden structures are to be seen, especially on horse farms, but to the landscape lover these are unattractive. Protectors should be as unobtrusive as possible. The use of electric fences makes it feasible to have very lightweight, effective, cheap protection with the minimum of visual impact. Suitable electric protectors have been devised to deter almost all animals and because of their cheapness, ease of erection and effectiveness they are probably the best choice. To be sure there will be accidents, with the inevitable damage or even total loss of the trees, but this risk must be offset by the probability that the use of electric fences will enable many more trees to be planted in a season than if reliance is placed on mechanical protection. The odd loss out of a large planting is tolerable, and on balance more will be accomplished over the years by the use of electric fencing than by any other means. In any case there is plenty of evidence to show that many structures built of timber in one form or another merely act as convenient rubbing points for stock, eventually collapsing under the constant pressure being exerted by animals weighing half a ton or more.

Landholders must make their choice according to their own experience and inclinations, so there are no firm recommendations on what the protector should look like. [Any kind of fencing material can be used to encircle the tree far enough from the trunk to protect roots and immature trees from animal damage. Trees are susceptible to damage until the crown of the tree reaches a sufficient height where animals cannot reach these tempting leaves or needles for nibbles. Don't build a protector that's too small and will thus restrict the growth of the trunk.]

Special mention should be made of the best use of land so that grazing loss is minimal; in this respect corners should not be overlooked. There are already two fences erected and it is little effort to wire up between the two to complete the triangle. If the line is taken across from points 23 feet (7 meters) from the corner, it will be approximately 33 feet (10 meters) long. This enclosed area will be .0025 of a hectare (about 1/120 of an acre). Each such area could hold anything from three to six trees and would hardly be missed on even the smallest farm. This is especially so in paddocks which are mostly used for cropping, where the headlands are lost to production anyway.

Some protectors provide excellent scratching facilities.

Site Preparation

Trees do not thrive in competition with grass--especially farm pastures which tend to be well established and vigorous. A new tree can get away to a good start if planting is carried out in accordance with principles set out in this chapter, but may well succumb to summer stress if it has to compete with grass for moisture. Even before summer, small seedlings can be overwhelmed by spring grass flushes; these will have long been awaited and needed on other parts of the farm but in the planting area may well result in the seedlings never being seen again. Farmers are busy people in the spring and even with the best of intentions often never get back to planting sites to release trees from competitive growth. So plan your plantings in such a way that they can cope without assistance for several months, for your animals will, and certainly should, take priority.

Before planting, the grass sward should be removed by very close cropping or preferably spraying with a non-residual herbicide which with the addition of Simazine will be effective for several months. This may in itself not be enough, since at planting time in the winter such vigorous grasses as kikuyu, bermuda and dallisgrass are dormant and will appear again during the summer. Small plants do not stand a chance against fast, tall-growing species. Post-planting treatment is therefore necessary for at least the summer following planting, and with slower growing species it could well be necessary for some years after planting if best results are to be obtained.

Having selected a suitable tree for your site, or vice versa, and erected a protector, you then have to plant the tree which you have bought to match those conditions. Ideally you should follow the guidelines set out here.

Peat moss improves texture of heavy soils and provides fiber to assist moisture in light soils.

Farmers must pay special attention to new trees for they are not planted in the sheltered suburb of a city. A farmer is transferring a plant from a protected, pampered nursery environment to exposed and often harsh conditions of the fields. It cannot just be dropped in a hole and forgotten. It must be nurtured if it is to become strong, healthy and grow rapidly to maturity.

If you can think far enough ahead it is good sense to dig your holes before collection of the plants from the nursery: cut off the turf, dig a hole, chop up the turf, and replace all back in the hole making sure you do not bring the subsoil up to the surface. It will break down with the colder weather and will be easy to handle at planting time. If you have the opportunity, it is helpful to mix heavy subsoil with peat moss, sand or old farm manure to help make it more acceptable to the new root system. Adding fibrous material to very light soil improves moisture retention. Just before planting is a good time to use your herbicide to knock down any regrowth. If conditions are very wet it is better to wait until they have improved (unless it is permanently wet when the problem has to be handled on a permanent basis), and if conditions are unduly windy, some artificial shelter such as plastic mesh, old straw bales, etc. will help early establishment.

Drainage

If a planting hole cannot drain it acts as a tank, keeping soil in the root zone saturated and shutting off air. Failure through root rot is almost inevitable. Common sense dictates the most appropriate methods to solve the problem: penetrating the impermeable layer with a posthole digger or crowbar, adding a side drain, cutting radiating straight lines from the planting hole, digging an oversize hole and backfilling with 2/3rds of soil mixed with coarse material, or just giving up and building a pond instead.

Deep cuts help disperse moisture into the surrounding soil.

Bare Root Planting

In winter and spring bare-rooted trees are usually available from nurseries and are cheaper than container-grown plants. Bare-rooted trees are usually easier to handle and more vigorous, so winter planting is not only of benefit to the plants but usually coincides with the quieter time on the farm. When bare-rooted trees are planted the hole is back-filled with a uniform soil mix similar to the surrounding soil. By contrast a container-grown plant has two different mixtures in the hole, often making it unfirm and water penetration difficult, as well as forcing the roots to adapt to a radical change of environment.

Bare-rooted plants need to have fresh plump roots which are not dry and withered, looking as if they have had a long day out! If they do not look fresh and healthy do not buy them, but if you have the misfortune to have them in such a condition then give them a good soaking.

Whenever you are planting, care in handling is vital. Do not let the roots or the foliage dry out, and at all times protect the whole plant from the wind. If you allow foliage to get in the wind, desiccation will result at a time when the roots are dormant and total loss is more than likely. Don't just heave your new purchases on the back of the pickup along with the posts, wire and bags of stockfeed, for they will surely suffer physical damage. Out of the nursery into an 80 km/hour (50 mph) gale is no fun for young trees. Put them into some sort of container and make sure it is big enough, for young roots are easily damaged.

The planting hole should be large enough to accommodate all the roots without cramping, bending or cutting them. The tree should be planted at the same level as it was in the nursery, and this is

Before planting, soak trees in water for 5 minutes, or until bubbles stop rising. Drain surplus water.

clearly indicated by soil marks on the stem. Soils should be firmly compacted around the roots (this does not mean jumping up and down on the backfill using your heel in like manner to a post rammer). Leave the top surface soil loose as this helps to absorb water. An after-planting watering is a good idea if this is practical.

For the forest species such as pines, eucalypts, etc. it is equally important that seedlings be of the highest quality--more so in fact since once planted they are likely to receive less attention than the amenity species, since they are planted in such large numbers.

Preconditioning in the nursery is now a highly specialized technique. Land owners establishing woodlots should ensure that nursery handling, uplifting and transport to the site are of the highest standards. You are recommended to make purchases only from established and reliable nurseries experienced in growing such species.

Container-Grown Trees

These are popular because they extend the planting season and can be held over between nursery sale and planting time without any adverse effect. When buying make sure the plant looks healthy, has a vigorous robust appearance and good foliage.

Carefully remove containers without damaging the roots.

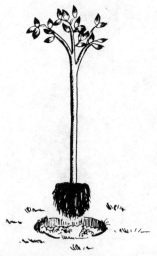

Do not disturb the root ball except to straighten or disentangle roots from the container.

Watch for root-bound plants and avoid those where roots can be seen growing through drainage holes or above soil level. Plastic bags, cans or pots must be removed with minimum disturbance of the root ball. Plants in solid containers can be tipped upside down on the hand, with the tree stem held between the fingers, and the edge tapped on a post or spade. Burlap should not be removed if young shoots are strongly growing through it. If this has happened cut the twine, pull the hessian away from the bark only and leave it to rot in the ground.

Dig a hole twice the size of the container. Container plants are often grown in a light fast-draining mix that favors rapid root development, and if set into small holes the roots may well find it difficult to penetrate the surrounding material. This will make them shallow rooted and liable to dry out. Your large hole should be back filled with good friable easily penetrated soil mix which will make life easy for the plant which has just had to suffer a major change in its environment.

Basic planting technique is similar to bare-rooted and again you should not plant too deeply--the top of the root ball should not be more than 1.2 inches (3 cm) below the soil. After removing the container have a good look at the roots. If they are crowded or

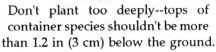

Don't plant too deeply--tops of container species shouldn't be more than 1.2 in (3 cm) below the ground.

Staking stabilizes trees during establishment period. Position before planting to lessen root damage.

all coiled up, straighten them out with a knife just before insertion in the hole. Surplus roots which have spiralled round until they look like the inside of a clock should be cut off so that any new growth will go sideways and downwards into fresh ground. Plants which are grown in peat pots can be planted, container and all, but make sure that the bottom of the pot is broken apart to facilitate easy root penetration. It is also most important to remove the lip of the pot or cover it with soil, otherwise it will act as a wick and allow moisture to evaporate into the atmosphere with disastrous results.

Staking

For larger specimens a stake will stabilize a tree and will help establishment since it prevents the movement that breaks off new roots, and assists in training the tree to a good shape. In wetter spots it is essential if a larger specimen is to stay even reasonably upright. The stake should preferably be placed in position prior to planting to prevent root damage. The tree should be placed on the leeward side and secured firmly with a flexible tie--don't buy one as there is no more useful end to the life of pantyhose than to support a tree in its infancy. Old bicycle tubes can be made into good ties, but periodic checks should always be made to ensure that there is no strangling.

Tie-on labels attached at the nursery can cause ring barking, so always remove them and retie them to the stake if on-site identification is desired.

Transplanting

Sometimes a tree larger than is usually handled needs to be moved; for instance a cedar might have grown too large for the home garden and has to be moved out on to the farm.

Plan to move the tree during winter when it is dormant. Several months beforehand dig around the tree with the spade vertical, cutting downwards near the drip line. This will shorten the outer roots and encourage the growth of more compact feeder roots.

A few days before moving, soak the whole root mass with water and spray the leaves. Prepare the planting hole as described earlier, making quite sure it is large enough. Choose a calm cloudy day if possible.

Dig a trench around the tree, then gradually sever the roots under the root ball, being careful not to crumble the soil away. An alternative method of wrenching is to cut the roots on three sides only about a month before moving the tree. At transplanting time the remaining roots are cut. This method could be used if the tree is to be moved at relatively short notice. Tie a rag or something similar onto a branch facing North.

Wrap sacking around the root ball, draw up tightly and secure firmly, especially underneath where the soil is liable to fall away from the roots.

When replanting in the new site ensure that the rag is positioned to the North. This reduces one cause of stress to the tree by not altering its orientation.

Work as quickly as possible following earlier planting directions. Larger trees require thorough watering several times during the first year after moving.

Mulching

This is a great help to young plants and consists of a 2.5-3 inch (6-8cm) layer of material around them. It acts as an insulator, prevents moisture evaporation and keeps roots at an even temperature. It also stops the soil surface from baking into a hard pan. Most importantly it acts as a weed control. The ground should be soaked before applying mulch. Ideally peat moss could be applied around especially valuable specimens, but this is hardly feasible for large-scale plantings on farms. On the other hand, the person on the land often has access to many suitable materials such as old hay, sawdust from the mobile mill, post peelings from post thinning, hedge trimmings from the horticulture block, or home garden, or garden compost and leaf mould. Mulches

Mulching prevents weeds and lessens moisture evaporation. Soak the ground well before mulching.

must be kept away from the trunk as excess heat and moisture contained in the material can destroy the bark. Mulching is one of those tasks which is avoidable and seemingly of doubtful worth at the time of application since there are many other things which seem more important, but it will pay very handsome dividends.

Fertilizer

Excessive feeding at planting time is both dangerous and unnecessary. A natural fertilizer such as blood and bone can be incorporated into the soil before planting, but the safest way is to scatter a couple of handfuls onto the surface after planting. By the time it reaches the roots it will be in soluble form and readily available. The farmer, however, can usually find organic manure about the farm. What better than animal dung, which serves as a mulch as well as manure? For centuries trees have grown adequately without any artificial manures. Seeds have simply germinated and grown, so why hurry to grow at accelerated speeds? One must learn to accept that if a tree is planted on a site resembling its natural conditions, then it will grow fast enough to be quite rewarding to the planter.

Watering

It is impractical for the farmer to maintain a regular watering program. Therefore, it is even more important to take steps at planting to minimize competition for moisture. Elimination of weeds, good site preparation and mulching are the answers. However, there will be some specimen trees that deserve that extra bit of attention. They may be planted near the home or sheds where there are watering points. These should be given additional water during that first summer when stress is likely to be greatest.

Avoid excessive feeding of fertilizer at planting. A couple of handfuls on the soil surface will be in soluble form by the time it eventually reaches the roots.

"A little and often" is an adage that can kill the tree when applied to a watering program. The water will never penetrate to the lower levels. The result will be a shallow root system. Water moves very little laterally so enough must be used each time to give coverage of the whole root zone, i.e. water out to the drip line. Over-watering, particularly in heavy clay, will be worse than not watering at all, for the roots will drown through lack of oxygen. The following watering guide suggests days between applications:

	Sand	Loam	Clay
Shallow Rooted	4-6	7-10	10-12
Medium	7-10	10-15	15-20
Deep Rooted	15-20	20-30	30 or more

Conditions other than those in the soil will also influence the degree of moisture stress, a major one being the desiccating effect of wind, which will increase water demand. A system used in Israel for centuries can be effective when stones or small rocks are available. These are put into a layer or two in a depression around the base of the young tree, acting as a mulch and through condensation providing that extra drop of moisture. Another de-

vice is a plastic bag that can trickle feed water at a preset, controlled rate. It also acts as a mulch and can be reused--just the job for a busy farmer or anyone who fancies a little yachting during the heat of the summer. Water may well come from the farm bore, but to most people putting it on plants is the bore and should be avoided if possible. The plant will be stronger and more independent if it is grown in conditions which will enable it to cope on its own. Make that extra effort at planting time and so lessen your post-planting work.

Give a thorough watering at planting time and regular soakings during dry weather.

North American Notes

The American Arborvitae (*Thuja occidentalis*) was the first tree imported into North America from Europe. It was called the "Tree of Life" or Arborvitae when it saved the lives of explorer Jacques Cartier's crew who had become stricken with scurvy during their Canadian expedition. Swampy cedar woods provide winter shelter for deer. The Atlantic White Cedar (*Chamaecyparis thyoides*), Western Redcedar (*Thuja plicata*) provide excellent browse for deer.

8: Wood Properties

The table that follows is to be used as a quick guide to indicate the qualities of some of the wood that could be available from trees that grow in North America. The list is by no means definitive, but is intended to give you food for thought. It must be strongly emphasized that the figures in this table should not be used as a reliable base for making decisions, which might involve considerable financial outlay. Evaluations of the wood have been made by different organizations using different criteria, for instance, the ability to accept treatment may have been assessed with or without the use of pressure, and the sizes of the pieces treated may have varied from small 2 inch by 2 inch (50 mm x 50 mm) test stakes to 8 inch (200 mm) round posts. Similarly, when measuring ground durability, this proviso could apply.

The purpose of including such information here is to encourage people to look a little further into possible end uses of surplus timber before condemning it to the firewood heap. If it is not one of the better known hardwoods, there is a tendency to almost automatically bulldoze unwanted trees over the bank or into a firewood heap.

Our research indicates that almost every tree listed in this book produces worthwhile usable timber, which is valued by the people of the native country in which it grows. Wood is a resource that we discard very carelessly, but there is often a good on-farm use for lowly-regarded trees that are no longer required. For instance, *Chamaecyparis lawsoniana* (Lawson or Port Orford Cypress) shelterbelts were at one time extensively planted in New Zealand, but due to poor management and deterioration through canker thousands of trees of good straight form have been ripped out. Almost all of them have been or are still being burned. In its home states of Oregon and California the timber is highly prized and becoming more so because the supply is now limited. The timber can be used on the farm, for it has a life of at least 11-15 years in the ground, probably much longer, and is suitable for poles for temporary horticulture shelter required during the period when permanent live shelter is growing to effective size.

Many unwanted trees have attributes that make the timber well worth processing, although it is acknowledged that getting such logs sawn up is not always easy. The dominance of pine in the whole industry has resulted in a high degree of disinterest by millers generally in the "one off" log, which a farmer is likely to want processed. But as values of better-known hardwoods go on increasing--their scarcity will inevitably cause this--milling of good quality logs may well be worthwhile even if you feel you are being cheated in the process. The worth of the operation must be measured against current milling prices. A mobile sawmiller will often do a lot of work for a quarter the cost. A well-grown old plane, chestnut or oak tree could contain 70-105 cubic feet (2-3 cubic meters) of timber, so do some sums before you too readily condemn it to the scrap heap. You may well find that you or your friends will acquire some attractive and unusual paneling or interesting furniture lengths.

The table is thus to be used with discretion but offers a guide to the enthusiast who often wonders what he or she can do with a tree that has finished its useful life.

Notes

Density: The weight of a piece of wood clearly varies with the amount of water that it contains. When the weight is mentioned as a means of measuring density, the moisture content should be stated. Most authorities use 12% as this is an acceptable content for satisfactory woodworking. However in many cases information on average weights of timbers has been taken from sources where moisture content is not stated, but one must assume that it is around the 12% mark. In all species a considerable variation in weight is found to occur, apart from differences arising from moisture content.

Natural Durability: Assessment is always based on heartwood, and sapwood is classed as perishable. Natural durability is of importance when timber is exposed to dampness, i.e. above about 20% moisture content, thus is of vital importance when in contact with the ground. Decay resistance of most timbers varies, even in pieces cut from the same tree, so durability has to be assessed in approximate terms. Most authorities use a standard five grading system based on 2 inch x 2 inch (50mm x 50mm) pieces. Larger sizes will last longer. For example, a piece 4 inches x 4 inches (100mm x 100mm) will last about twice as long as the 2 inch x 2 inch. The expected service is measured in ground-contact situations, but if the same timber is used in an above-ground situation then it would be reasonably safe to move its life up to the next classification.

Grade of Durability		Approximate Life in Ground Contact
Perishable	(P)	Less than 5 years
Non-Durable	(ND)	5-10 years
Moderately Durable	(MD)	10-15 years
Durable	(D)	15-25 years
Very Durable	(VD)	More than 25 years

Treatability: The ease with which a non-durable timber can be impregnated with preservatives depends on its permeability. Some timbers are virtually impenetrable, but it is well to remember that round wood is often surrounded by the more perishable sapwood that is easily treatable, thus roundwood can often be treated for use as posts where sawn timber from the same tree would not be treatable.

It would be useful if sufficient information were available to expand this table to itemize sapwood treatability of various species as distinct from heartwood. Unfortunately most sources of information do not distinguish between the two. A species with a durable heartwood and treatable sapwood is likely to be ideal for ground contact use, whereas a species with untreatable sapwood should possibly have this removed. This would decrease the strength properties of the roundwood because machine peeling or shaving can reduce total pole strength by about 40%.

There are various methods of pressure treatment using different preservatives, but the resistance of a timber impregnation under pressure will generally be of the same order whatever type of preservative is used.

Simple diffusion treatment is possible with all species when used on freshly cut green wood, thus the tables relate only to the pressure treatment of dry wood.

Permeable (P): Can be penetrated completely under pressure and can usually be heavily impregnated by hot and cold open tank process.

Moderately Resistant (MR): Usually fairly easy to treat, but often there are some problems with specific species.

Resistant (R): Not amenable--difficult to obtain any worthwhile impregnation even after prolonged treatment.

CAUTION: Because of the variability within species, the differences in growing conditions from country to country, and the varying techniques that have been used in assessing the timber qualities, it is unwise to embark on any large-scale project without discussing it further with the appropriate experts. This information is given in good faith and has been obtained from what are believed to be reliable sources.

	density air dried kg/cu m	durability	treatability (pressure treatment of dry wood)
Abies			
amabilis (Silver Fir)	420	ND	
concolor (White Fir)	400	ND	
grandis (Grand Fir)	450	ND	R
magnifica (Red Fir)	470	MD	
procera (Noble Fir)	420	ND	R
Acer			
macrophyllum (Bigleaf Maple)	540	ND	
negundo (Ashleaf Maple)	420		
nigrum (Black Maple)	700	ND	MR
pseudoplatanus (Sycamore)	610	P	P
rubrum (Red Maple)	600	ND	
saccharum (Sugar Maple)	720	ND	MR
Aesculus			
hippocastanum (Horsechestnut)	510	P	P
Ailanthus			
altissima (Tree-of-Heaven)	600		
Alnus			
rubra (Red Alder)	600	ND	
Betula			
lutea (Yellow Birch)	690	P	MR
papyrifera (Paper Birch)	620	ND	MR
Calocedrus			
decurrens (Incense-Cedar)	400		
Carya			
cordiformis (Bitternut Hickory)	750	ND	MR
glabra (Pignut Hickory)	850	ND	MR
illinoiensis (Pecan)	730	ND	MR
laciniosa (Shellbark Hickory)	760	ND	MR
ovata (Shagbark Hickory)	1000	ND	MR
tomentosa (Mockernut Hickory)	800	ND	MR

	density air dried kg/cu m	durability	treatability (pressure treat- ment of dry wood)
Casuarina			
equisetifolia(HorsetailCasuarina)	900	MD	R
Catalpa			
bignonioides (Common Catalpa)		ND	
speciosa (Catawba-Tree)	400	D	
Cedrus			
deodara (Deodar Cedar)	560	MD	R
Chamaecyparis			
lawsoniana (Port Orford-Cedar)	470	MD	R
nootkatensis (Alaska Cedar)	500	D	R
thyoides (Atlantic White Cedar)	360	D	
Cinnamomum			
camphora (Camphortree)	640	MD	
Cupressus			
arizonica (Arizona Cypress)		D	
macrocarpa (Monterey Cypress)	500	MD	R
Diospyros (Persimmon)	800		
Fagus			
grandifolia (Beech)	720	ND	
Fraxinus			
americana (White Ash)	660	P	P
Gleditsia			
triacanthos (Honey Locust)	700	D	
Grevillea			
robusta (Silk-Oak)	610	MD	MR

	density air dried kg/cu m	durability	treatability (pressure treatment of dry wood)
Juglans			
nigra (Black Walnut)	640	D	
regia (English Walnut)	640	MD	R
Juniperus			
communis (Common Juniper)	500		
virginiana (Eastern Redcedar)	530	D	
Larix			
decidua (European Larch)	560	ND-MD	R
laricina (American Larch)	560	MD	R
occidentalis (Western Larch)	610	MD	R
Liquidambar			
styraciflua (Sweetgum)	550		
Liriodendron			
tulipifera (Tulip-Tree)	480	ND	R
Maclura			
pomifera (Osage-Orange)	760	D	
Magnolia			
grandiflora (Bull Bay Magnolia)	560	ND	
Malus (Crabapple)	750		
Melia			
azedarach (Chinaberry)	500	D	
Morus			
alba (White Mulberry)	640		
Paulownia			
tomentosa (Princess-Tree)	c300	MD	

	density air dried kg/cu m	durability	treatability (pressure treat- ment of dry wood)
Picea			
abies (Norway Spruce)	470	P	R
pungens (Blue Spruce)		Prob. P	R
sitchensis (Sitka Spruce)	430	ND	R
Pinus			
contorta (Lodgepole Pine)	520	ND	R
monticola (Western White Pine)	420	ND	MR
muricata (Bishop Pine)	490	ND	Variable
ponderosa (Arizona Pine)	460	ND	R
radiata (Monterey Pine)	480	ND	Variable
strobus (White Pine)	370	ND	Variable
sylvestris (Scotch Pine)	510	ND	MR
Platanus			
acerifolia (London Plane)	620	ND	
orientalis (Oriental Plane)	640	ND	
Populus			
alba (White Poplar)	400-450	ND	P
deltoides (Eastern Cottonwood)	400-450	ND	P
nigra "Italica" (Lombardy Poplar)	400-450	ND	MR
tremuloides (Quaking Aspen)	400-450	ND	P
trichocarpa (Black Cottonwood)	400-450	ND	P
Pseudotsuga			
menziesii (Common Douglas Fir)	480	ND	R
Prunus spp. (Plum)	500-600		
Pyrus spp. (Pear)	700		
Quercus			
alba (White Oak)	750	D	R
coccinea (Scarlet Oak)	750		
rubra (Red Oak)	770	ND	MR

	density air dried kg/cu m	durability	treatability (pressure treatment of dry wood)
Robinia			
pseudoacacia (Black Locust)	720	VD	R
Salix spp. (Willow)	340-500	P	R
Sequoia			
sempervirens (Redwood)	400	MD	MR
Sequoiadendron			
giganteum (Giant Sequoia)	350?		
Taxodium			
distichum(AmericanBaldcypress)	510	D	MR
Thuja			
occidentalis (N. White Cedar)	340	D	R
plicata (Western Redcedar)	370	D	R
Tilia			
americana (Am. Basswood)	420	ND	P
Tsuga			
canadensis (Eastern Hemlock)	470	ND	R
heterophylla (Western Hemlock)	490	ND	R
Ulmus			
americana (American Elm)	560	ND	MR
glabra (Witch Elm)	670	ND	R
procera (English Elm)	550	ND	MR

9: Tree Selection

The following lists contain the genus names only. It is again emphasized that consulting your local nursery is advisable to ensure that what you buy matches your particular site conditions. This book is only an introduction to farm planting--additional homework is required to ensure success or at least to minimize failure.

Deciduous Trees for Autumn Color

Acer	Gleditsia	Quercus
Ailanthus	Juglans	Sorbus
Betula	Larix	Taxodium
Carya	Liquidambar	Tilia
Diospyros	Liriodendron	Ulmus
Fagus	Nyssa	
Fraxinus	Populus	

Trees for Dry Sites

Acacia	Cupressus	Quercus
Acer	Eucalyptus	Robinia
Ailanthus	Gleditsia	Schinus
Albizia	Juniperus	Tamarix
Brachychiton	Maclura	
Casuarina	Pinus	

Tress for Damp Sites

Acacia	Cupressus	Populus
Acer	Eucalyptus	Pyrus
Alnus	Fraxinus	Quercus
Betula	Larix	Salix
Carya	Liquidambar	Sequoia
Casuarina	Liriodendron	Taxodium
Catalpa	Nyssa	
Chamaecyparis	Picea	

Trees with Fragrant Flowers & Foliage

Flowers	Foliage
Acacia	Calocedrus
Aesculus	Cedrus
Fruit trees	Cinnamomum
Magnolia	Cupressus
Malus	Eucalyptus
Robinia	Juglans
Tilia	Pinus
	Populus

Trees for Coastal Planting

This section has been divided into two parts (1) those trees known to withstand constant salt-laden winds and (2) trees recommended by some authorities as being suitable for seaside conditions, but which will not necessarily withstand strong winds. These could be well worth trying if the sites are reasonably sheltered and the climate appropriate.

Trees for Exposed Coastal Sites

Cupressus	Pinus	Tamarix

Trees for Sheltered Coastal Sites

Acacia	Grevillea	Salix
Alnus	Liquidambar	Sequoia
Carpinus	Melia	Sophora
Castanea	Paulownia	Sorbus
Casuarina	Populus	Thuja
Cinnamomum	Pseudotsuga	Ulmus
Eucalyptus	Quercus	

"I see tree planting as a sign that the farm is mature and stable. People are dedicated to the land and certain they'll be there for a long time. They've solved most of the day-to-day problems, and are now fine tuning the system and investing in the future. If your farm fits this description, perhaps next spring is the time to get started planting trees."

Eric Ronneberg
Forest Resource Center
Lanesboro, Minnesota

Glossary

Accumulator plants: Those plants which have an ability to collect trace elements from the soil with storage in their tissues of several hundred times the amount contained in an equal weight of soil.

Agroforestry: The intentional blending of agricultural crops and/or livestock on the same land with tree crops. The goal of this type of agriculture is to increase and diversify the total production of a given area of land while simultaneously improving and conserving the land.

Agro-silviculture: An agroforestry system that deals with the production of agriculture and forestry crops.

Agro-silvo-pastoralism: An agroforestry system combining the production of agricultural and forestry crops with livestock.

Browse: Any woody plant short enough for animals to reach its leaves for food.

Clear-cut or clear-cutting forestry: Harvesting trees from a site in which everything is cut to ground level.

Clearwood: Wood without knots.

Coppice: Young regrowth on a cut tree or bush.

Dry matter: Forage after the moisture has been removed. As a measure it is generally noted in tons per acre as TDM.

Fan-pruning: Pruning of branches growing at right angles to the line of the shelterbelt. This system is akin to trimming, but branches are removed flush with the stem.

Mast: The fruit of a tree.

Mattock: A farm tool with the blade positioned at right angles to the handle, and is used for loosening soil and digging up roots.

Multipurpose forest: The regeneration and management of trees to produce not only wood, but leaves and/or fruit that are suitable for food and/or fiber.

Pruning: Removing all branches up the stem of the tree to a determined height.

Paperwood or pulpwood: Trees for the manufacture of paper.

Riparian zone: The area alongside a stream.

Silvo-pastoralism: An agroforestry system that deals with the production of wood and livestock.

Stems (per acre): The number of trees in an acre.

Subsoiling: Using a ripper, or curved-shank plow to cut into the soil for air and water penetration.

TDM: Tons of dry matter per acre.

Bibliography

General References:
Collingwood, G.H. & Brush, W.D. *Knowing your Trees*. The American Forestry Assn., 1974.
Constantine, Albert, Jr. *Know Your Woods*. Charles Scribner's Sons, 1975.
Evans, B. *Revegetation Manual*. Queen Elizabeth II National Trust, 1983.
Edlin, H.L. and Nimmo, M. *The World of Trees*. Orbis Publishing, 1974.
Gorer, Richard. *Illustrated Guide to Trees*. Kingfisher Books, 1980.
Handbook of Hardwoods. Her Majesty's Stationery Office, 1972.
Handbook of Softwoods. Her Majesty's Stationery Office, Second Edition, 1977.
Harrison, Richmond E. *Handbook of Trees & Shrubs*. A.H., & A.W. Reed, Wellington, 1974.
Hillier's Manual of Trees & Shrubs. David & Charles, Revised Edition, 1974.
Leathart, Scott. *Trees of the World*. Hamlyn, 1977.
McWhannell, F.B. *Eucalypts for New Zealand Farms, Parks and Gardens*, Pauls Book Arcade, 1960.
Macoboy, Stirling. *What Tree is That?* Landsdowne Press, 1979.
Phillips, Roger. *Trees of North America and Europe*. Random House, 1978.
Rendle, B.J. *World Timbers*. 3 Vols., Earnest Benn Ltd., 1969.
Stockley, George. *Trees Farms and the New Zealand Landscape*, Northern Southland Farm Forestry Assn., 1973
Sunset Western Garden Book. 1967.

Planting Design
Brian Clouston (ed.), *Landscape Design with Plants*. The Landscape Institute. Heinemann, London, 1977.
Sylvia Crowe, *The Landscape of Forests and Woods*. Forestry Commission Booklet 44. H.M.S.O., London, 1978.
D.S.I.R., Land Alone Endures: *Land Use and the Role of Research*. Discussion Paper No. 3, Government Printer, 1980.
Boyden Evans, *Revegetation Manual: Using New Zealand Native Plants*. QE II National Trust, 1983.
Diane Lucas, *Landscape Guidelines for Rural South Canterbury*. 1980-81.
B. Mollison, D. Holmgren, *Permaculture One: A Perennial Agriculture for Human Settlements*. Corgi, Australia, 1978.
B. Mollison, *Permaculture Two: Practical Design for Town and Country Permanent Agriculture*. Tagari, Australia, 1979.

New Zealand Forest Service, Landscape Section, *Creative Forestry: A Guideline for Forest Managers.* 1982.

Trees, Pasture and Soil
G.O. Eyles, "Distribution and severity of Present Soil Erosion in New Zealand." *NZ Geographer* Vol 39 No. 1. Apr. 1983.
Agroforestry Farming Research at Tikitere. NZ Forest Service Handbook 1993.
    (This handbook includes a full list of relevant literature on the subject).
NZ Farm Forestry Journal Vol 20 No. 4 1978.
Streamland 3. National Water and Soil Conservation Organization 1982.

Shelter
J.M. Caborn, "Shelterbelts and Windbreaks," Dept Forestry and National Resources, University of Edinburgh, 1965.
C.G.R. Chavasse, "Management of Shelterbelts for Wood Products," *NZ Journal of Forestry* 27 (2), 1982.
R.L. Hathaway, "New and Potential Horticultural Shelter Species," *NZ Agricultural Science* 16 (1), 1982.
R.L. Hathaway, "Back to Basics on Shelter," *Growing Today*, July 1983.
J.J. Lynch, CSIRO Division of Plant Industry Annual Report, 1972/73.
J.J. Lynch, CSIRO Division of Plant Industry Annual Report, 1973/74.
Ministry of Agriculture and Fisheries Information Service M.A.F. Aglinks on Shelter, FPP 385, 390, 441; HPP 62, 120, 121, 130, 131, 137, 167, 169, 170, 184, 205, 227.
NZ Forest Service, NZ Forest Service Policy on Exotic Special Purpose Species (1981).
I. Nicholas, "Timber Production from Shelterbelts," Forest Research Report, 1982.
J.E. Radcliffe, "Grassland Responses to Shelter--A Review." *NZ Journal of Experimental Agriculture*, Vol 11: 5-10, 1983.
P.W. Smail, "Trees for Shelter," *Farm Forestry*, Vol 21-1, 1979.
J.W. Sturrock, "Shelter Boosts Crop Yield by 35%," *NZ Journal Agriculture*, Sept 1981.
J.W. Sturrock, "The Control of Wind: The Roles of Research and Farm Forestry," DSIR, Lincoln.

Shade
T.E. Bond and D.B. Laster, "Influence of Shading on Production of Midwest Feedlot Cattle." Transactions of ASAE Paper No. 74.4536, Aug. 1975.
J.W. Fuquay, *Journal of Animal Science*, Vol. 52 No. 1, 1981.

J. Hancock, "Direct Influence of Climate on Milk Production." Commonwealth Bureau of Dairy Science 16, 1954.

E.H. McIlvain and M.C. Shoop, "Shade for Improving Cattle Gains and Rangeland Use." Study conducted on the Southern Plains Experimental Range, Woodward, Oklahoma, by the Crops Research Division, Agricultural Research Service, U.S. Department of Agriculture. *Journal of Range Management*, Vol. 24 No. 3, May 1971.

Shingoro Moda, "The Feeding and Management of Farm Animals under Hot Weather Conditions." Extension Bulletin No. 27, Food and Fertilizer Technology Centre, Taiwan.

Peacock et al., "Influence of Shade on Fattening Cattle in South Florida." Bulletin 700 (Technical), Agricultural Experiment Stations, Institute of Food and Agricultural Sciences, University of Florida.

Birds
NZ Wildlife Service, "Tree Planting for Native Birds."

Bees
MAF Aglinks FPP 529 and 530

Wood Properties
Building Research Establishment, Princes Risborough Laboratory, *Handbook of Hardwoods*. Her Majesty's Stationery Office.

Handbook of Softwoods, as above.

Collingwood and Brush, *Knowing Your Trees*. The American Forestry Assn.

Albert Constantine Jr., *Know Your Woods*. Charles Scribner's Sons.

Hall Johnston and Chippendale, *Forest Trees of Australia*. Australian Government Publishing Service.

B.J. Rendle, *World Timbers*. Earnest Benn Ltd.

[NZ] Forest Research Institute, *The Natural Durability of Untreated Timbers*. What's New In Forest Research No. 112.

McQuire, Butcher, Hedley and Vinden, *Wood Preservation for the Farmer*. NZ Forest Service reprint 1277 O.D.C. 84.

NZ Institute of Foresters, *Forestry Handbook*.

In cross checking species that grow in North America:
Allen J. Coombes. *Eyewitness Handbooks Trees*. Dorling Kindersley, Inc. New York, 1992.

Wilbur H. and Marion B. Duncan. *Trees of the Southeastern United States*. The University of Georgia Press, Athens, 1988.

Roger Tory Peterson and George A. Petrides, *A Field Guide to Trees and Shrubs, Northeastern and north-central United States and southeastern and south-central Canada.* Houghton Mifflin Company, New York, 1986

J. Russell Smith. *Tree Crops, A Permanent Agriculture.* Island Press. Covelo, California, 1987.

George A. Petrides, *Western Trees, Western United States and Canada.* Houghton Mifflin Company, New York, 1992.

About the Authors

John and Bunny Mortimer are well known in the Waikato and throughout New Zealand as practicing farm foresters with a commitment to the many values of trees and a complementary awareness of the need for sound conservation practices.

As originators of Hamilton's Westlands golf course, they were responsible for the extensive tree planting to which it owes much of its attraction. The land they now farm gives evidence of the economic and other advantages of exotic plantings, combined with a valued heritage of native trees, the latter now covenanted to the QEII National Trust.

Both authors are active in consulting work. John Mortimer is a past president of the New Zealand Farm Forestry Association and before that was president of the Waikato Branch for eleven years. John is also chairman of Honikiwi Forest Limited, a 600-acre intensively managed plantation forest, incorporating agroforestry principles.

Bunny is active in conservation organizations, was a Waipa county councillor for ten years and a director of the Queen Elizabeth II National Trust for seven years. She and John were joint winners of the 1980 Black and Decker Award for farm forestry.

Their activities in promoting the concepts of farm forestry, conservation, and wise land use were recognized in 1995 by each being awarded a Queen's Service Medal.

The Mortimers have nine children and live on the outskirts of Hamilton, New Zealand, where they formerly bred Charolais cattle, but now run dry stock while they concentrate on increasing the range of trees in their arboretum known as Taitua.

Resources

Consult your area local extension agent for advice on trees that will grow well in your climate and soils.

Order seedlings from state-operated or private nurseries. To avoid the rush, order early and purchase more than you need in order to select the hardiest seedlings in a group.

"Agroforestry Practices" by Tim Snell (Publ. F2000), available from The Kerr Center, Inc., PO Box 588, Hwy. 271 S., Poteau, OK 74953. (918) 647-9123. This 4-page report includes information on windbreaks, establishing agroforestry trees, suggestions for planting, a list of trees suitable for southeastern Oklahoma, and a reading list.

Tree Crops: A Permanent Agriculture by J. Russell Smith. Island Press. 410 pages. This book was first published in 1929, was reprinted in 1950, and was reissued in 1987 by Island Press. It is not as it sounds, a forestry book, but a unique forage book. Smith's idea was to plant nut- and bean-producing trees in pastures and harvest their crops with grazing animals. These tree crops could be grown on very steep soils and eliminate the farmer's need to plant erosive corn for his animals. Some of the forage-producing trees he covered were oak, Honey Locust, persimmon, mulberry, mesquite, pecan and chestnut.

The American Garden Guidebook by Everitt L. Miller and Jay S. Cohen. M. Evans & Co., Inc. 294 pages. This guide lists 339 of "the finest botanical gardens, parks, and arboreta of Eastern North America." Sites range from Maritime Canada to Southern Florida in 28 states and provinces, and can provide examples to study for integrating trees into your landscape.

Index

Pa$ture Profit$ With Stocker Cattle
by Allan Nation

America's first book on stocker grazing is written for those who want to get rich with a minimum of financial risk.

In **Pa$ture Profit$ With Stocker Cattle,** Allan Nation, editor of the **Stockman Grass Farmer,** illustrates his economic theories on stocker cattle by profiling Mississippi grazier, Gordon Hazard. Famous in national beef cattle circles for his penny-pinching ways, Hazard claims never to have lost a dime on stocker cattle in over 40 years of graziering. **Pa$ture Profit$ With Stocker Cattle** shows how Hazard has accumulated and stocked a 3000-acre ranch solely from retained stocker profits with no bank leverage.

"Truly outstanding, something no cattleman should be without--at least if he depends on grass for his sustenance."
Livestock Weekly

"Filled with good information on running a stocker cattle business, the book provides information that can be applied to improve business management techniques for other businesses as well." Small Farm Today

"(Nation) takes an altogether different view of stock raising, dealing with bankers, marketing, investment in equipment, etc., than most of us grew up with...If this book doesn't create controversy and spark some soul searching, particularly in the cattle business, both beef and dairy, it isn't for lack of effort on the part of the author."
Draft Horse Journal

Pa$ture Profit$ With Stocker Cattle
ISBN: 0-9632460-0-3
Softcover 192 pages $24.95 + shipping and handling

Grass Farmers
by Allan Nation

If you're tired of reading farm stories of doom and gloom, bankruptcies and despair, then **Grass Farmers** will tell you about the many people who are making an excellent living on the land.

37 thought-provoking success stories tell
• how sheep dairying can produce a quality life from small acreages,
• how a grazier paid for his farm in six months,
• how to create a grass farm as a retirement job,
• how heifer grazing can give a grazier a mid-winter vacation,
• and much more, including a grazier's glossary.

Allan Nation has traveled the world studying and photographing grassland farming systems, profiled in this collection. Many of these stories appeared in now out-of-print editions of the **Stockman Grass Farmer**, where Nation has been editor since 1977.

"The book won't tell you how big to make your paddocks or when to move your stock. But it is a quick and inspirational read that could put many graziers on a path to higher profits."
New Farm

"We guarantee it will get you to thinking about new ways to increase your profit as a Grass Farmer."
Livestock Market Digest

"Interesting to see another face to farming. Great dream material." New England Farm Bulletin
Grass Farmers
ISBN: 0-9632460-1-1
Softcover, 192 pages. $23.50 + shipping and handling

Quality Pasture, How to create it, manage it, and profit from it
by Allan Nation

Do you know how to cut your current feed costs in half?

Quality Pasture, How to create it, manage it, and profit from it offers down-to-earth, low-cost tactics to create high-energy pasture that will reduce or eliminate expensive inputs or purchased feeds. **Quality Pasture** is the first book of its kind directed solely toward farmers like you who are beginning or practicing management-intensive grazing with ruminant livestock. Chapters cover:
● extending the grazing season during winter and summer slumps,
● matching stocking rates with pasture growth rate,
● how to create a drought management plan,
● tips for wet weather grazing,
● and a detailed section on making pasture silage.

Quality Pasture will walk you through the production model that can help you plug your profit leaks. Examples of real people making real profits show that quality pasture is not only possible, but can be profitable for you, too. Chapter summaries give you plenty of food for thought and action tips that you can begin using now.

"Among the people I admire most in agriculture are those who advocate new ideas and practices with unwavering conviction, passion and strength of will....Allan Nation speaks with the same passion he puts into his writing." **Successful Farming**

Quality Pasture
ISBN: 0-9632460-3-8
Softcover, 288 pages. $32.50 + shipping and handling

For a complete list of Green Park Press books and SGF Special Reports, request our FREE catalog.

Call 1-800-748-9808

Name _____

Address _____

City _____

State/Province _____ Zip/PostalCode _____

MC/VISA # _____ Expiration _____

Signature _____

Quantity	Title	Price Each	Sub Total
_____	Grass Farmers (weight 1 lb)	$23.50	_____
_____	Quality Pasture (weight 1 1/2 lbs)	$32.50	_____
_____	Pa$ture Profit$ With Stocker Cattle (1 lb)	$24.95	_____
_____	Free sample copy Stockman Grass Farmer magazine		
		Sub Total	_____
		Postage & Handling	_____
	Mississippi Residents Add 7% Sales Tax		_____

U.S. Funds Only, Please   **TOTAL:** _____

- -

Shipping:	Amount	Canada	Mexico
Under 2 lbs	$3.50	$5.50	$7.50
2-3 lbs	$4.75	$7.50	$12.00
3-4 lbs	$5.25	$8.50	$15.00
4-5 lbs	$6.50	$10.00	$16.75
5-6 lbs	$8.50	$11.75	$21.00
6-8 lbs	$12.00	$13.50	$24.00
8-10 lbs	$14.50	$16.75	$30.00

Foreign Postage: Add 35% of order.

Please make checks payable to:
Stockman Grass Farmer
PO Box 9607
Jackson, MS 39286-9607

1-800-748-9808
or 601-981-4805
FAX 601-981-8558

Green Park Press books and the **Stockman Grass Farmer** magazine are devoted solely to the art and science of turning pastureland into profits through the use of animals as nature's harvesters.

Green Park Press books and the Stockman Grass Farmer magazine are devoted solely to the art and science of turning pastureland into profits through the use of animals as nature's harvesters. To order a free sample copy of the magazine, or to purchase other Green Park Press titles:

Please make checks payable to:

Stockman Grass Farmer
PO Box 9607
Jackson, MS 39286-9607

1-800-748-9808
or 601-981-4805
FAX 601-981-8558

Shipping:	Amount	Canada	Mexico
Under 2 lbs	$3.50	$5.50	$7.50
2-3 lbs	$4.75	$7.50	$12.00
3-4 lbs	$5.25	$8.50	$15.00
4-5 lbs	$6.50	$10.00	$16.75
5-6 lbs	$8.50	$11.75	$21.00
6-8 lbs	$12.00	$13.50	$24.00
8-10 lbs	$14.50	$16.75	$30.00

Foreign Postage: Add 35% of order.

- -

Name _____

Address _____

City _____

State/Province _____ **Zip/Postal Code** _____

MC/VISA # _____ **Expiration** _____

Signature _____

Quantity	Title	Price Each	Sub Total
_____	Grass Farmers (weight 1 lb)	$23.50	_____
_____	Quality Pasture (weight 1 1/2 lbs)	$32.50	_____
_____	Pa$ture Profit$ With Stocker Cattle (1 lb)	$24.95	_____
_____	Free sample copy Stockman Grass Farmer magazine		

Sub Total _____

Postage & Handling _____

Mississippi Residents Add 7% Sales Tax _____

U.S. Funds Only, Please   **TOTAL:** _____

STOCKMAN GRASSFARMER
PO BOX 2300
RIDGELAND MS 39158
1-601-853-1861
1-800-748-9808

Name _____

Address _____

City _____

State/Province _____ Zip/PostalCode _____

MC/VISA # _____ Expiration _____

Signature _____

Quantity	Title	Price Each	Sub Total
_____	Grass Farmers (weight 1 lb)	$23.50	_____
_____	Quality Pasture (weight 1 1/2 lbs)	$32.50	_____
_____	Pa$ture Profit$ With Stocker Cattle (1 lb)	$24.95	_____
_____	Free sample copy Stockman Grass Farmer magazine		
		Sub Total	_____
		Postage & Handling	_____
	Mississippi Residents Add 7% Sales Tax		_____

U.S. Funds Only, Please   TOTAL: _____

- -

Shipping:	Amount	Canada	Mexico
Under 2 lbs	$3.50	$5.50	$7.50
2-3 lbs	$4.75	$7.50	$12.00
3-4 lbs	$5.25	$8.50	$15.00
4-5 lbs	$6.50	$10.00	$16.75
5-6 lbs	$8.50	$11.75	$21.00
6-8 lbs	$12.00	$13.50	$24.00
8-10 lbs	$14.50	$16.75	$30.00

Foreign Postage: Add 35% of order.

Please make checks payable to:
Stockman Grass Farmer
PO Box 9607
Jackson, MS 39286-9607

1-800-748-9808
or 601-981-4805
FAX 601-981-8558

Green Park Press books and the **Stockman Grass Farmer** magazine are devoted solely to the art and science of turning pastureland into profits through the use of animals as nature's harvesters.

Green Park Press books and the Stockman Grass Farmer magazine are devoted solely to the art and science of turning pastureland into profits through the use of animals as nature's harvesters. To order a free sample copy of the magazine, or to purchase other Green Park Press titles:

Please make checks payable to:

Stockman Grass Farmer
PO Box 9607
Jackson, MS 39286-9607

1-800-748-9808
or 601-981-4805
FAX 601-981-8558

Shipping:	Amount	Canada	Mexico
Under 2 lbs	$3.50	$5.50	$7.50
2-3 lbs	$4.75	$7.50	$12.00
3-4 lbs	$5.25	$8.50	$15.00
4-5 lbs	$6.50	$10.00	$16.75
5-6 lbs	$8.50	$11.75	$21.00
6-8 lbs	$12.00	$13.50	$24.00
8-10 lbs	$14.50	$16.75	$30.00

Foreign Postage: Add 35% of order.

- -

Name _____

Address _____

City _____

State/Province_____ Zip/Postal Code_____

MC/VISA # _____ Expiration _____

Signature _____

Quantity	Title	Price Each	Sub Total
_____	Grass Farmers (weight 1 lb)	$23.50	_____
_____	Quality Pasture (weight 1 1/2 lbs)	$32.50	_____
_____	Pa$ture Profit$ With Stocker Cattle (1 lb)	$24.95	_____
_____	Free sample copy Stockman Grass Farmer magazine		

Sub Total _____

Postage & Handling _____

Mississippi Residents Add 7% Sales Tax _____

U.S. Funds Only, Please   **TOTAL:** _____

STOCKMAN GRASSFARMER
PO BOX 2300
RIDGELAND MS 39158
1-601-853-1861
1-800-748-9808